Hill Song

Hill Song

A COUNTRY JOURNAL

Lee Pennock Huntington

Illustrations by Elfriede Abbe

The Countryman Press

Woodstock, Vermont

Countryman Classics are books of eloquence, charm, and literary quality that our editors wish to restore to print, in affordable new editions, for the enjoyment of successive generations of readers.

Note: Some names of people and places have been changed in order to protect their privacy.

L.P.H.

Library of Congress Cataloging-in-Publication Data
Huntington, Lee Pennock.
   Hill song.
   1. Country life — Vermont. 2. Vermont — Social life and customs. 3. Huntington, Lee Pennock — Homes and haunts — Vermont. I. Title.
F55.H86 1985   974.3'043'0924   85-16832
ISBN 0-88150-060-7

Designed by Leslie Fry
Illustrations by Elfriede Abbe
Printed in the United States of America

For
WILLIAM

For ye shall go out with joy, and be led forth with peace: the mountains and the hills shall break forth before you into singing, and all the trees of the field shall clap their hands.

Isaiah, 55:12

Contents

SPRING   *1*

SUMMER   *53*

AUTUMN   *87*

WINTER   *123*

Hill Song

Spring

On a brilliant March day all blazing light and radiant blue sky above the dazzling snowfields, the idea of ghosts pales into nothingness. Yet within the house the memory of them remains, not terrifyingly, only tinged with a respectful tenderness. They did belong here once, and if they have faded into silence and near-absence, that does not mean they may not come once more if they feel themselves called to protect the house. We don't believe it will be again in our time, but one can never be certain.

That the house might be haunted seemed a reasonable assumption the first time we saw it. It stood on the hill named for the man who had built it, the winds whistling through broken windows, rattling bleached blue shutters, lifting a corner of the rusty metal roof. On the thin old clapboards only traces of flaking ochre paint freckled the grey wood. The foundation stones were collapsing inward. Knee-high grass barricaded the doorway. A crone of a lilac bush bent its gnarled and broken limbs earthward.

Inside, crumbling plaster fell away, exposing the rough lath. Floors were splintered and rotten beneath a soapstone sink and a ruined black wood-range. Mice had left their punctuation marks on sagging shelves, squirrels had kept house in the attic, and there were starling nests in the cold chimneys.

It had been more than twenty years since the last Bartons had left this house, defeated by Depression losses and too many hard winters. An early snow the day of their departure had made the journey downhill a chancy thing. Henley Barton, his hand clenching the wheel of the balky old Ford truck, kept his eye on the treacherous road. Millie Barton, the five children huddled about her, looked back at the house where they had been born, and wept. This she told us many years later.

The place, some 200 acres, was sold to a neighboring dairy farmer who was interested in the hayfields and barns. The house itself was rented out for a time, but with no expenditures for maintenance it gradually decayed. Then it was hunters who came for a season to drink and sleep here around a pot-bellied stove, leaving their beer cans heaped in corners. Some of them used the great barn for target practice. In summer, lovers came to shelter in the empty bedrooms. Picnicking families explored pantry and cellar, children raced up and down stairs, making ghostnoises.

The real ghosts, the old Barton ghosts, retreated into the walls and cubby holes. Perhaps they slept. They had been around for a long time; they had, as the local saying goes, a right to be tired.

Thus it was when we first came to it. But we could see too that it had once been a house in which its owners had taken pride. It was masterfully sited, looking southward, encircled by other hills, set back from the dirt road so that one could see who was coming but not so close that anyone could look in the windows. It caught every bit of light all day long as the sun moved from the eastern hills to drop through Brandon Gap on the west.

The house fitted into its own hillside space, low, with steep roof and pleasant gables, a basic New England architecture out of Cape Cod. The great barn was to the north, the other barns and outbuildings ranging easterly. Maples and elms planted long ago defined the domestic area, and stone walls ran uphill, downhill, and crosswise along fields and pastures.

Everything was in disrepair, overgrown, sagging, disintegrating, bygone, yet everything spoke of a long human commitment to building and to husbandry. There was a serenity in the absolute solitude of the place, but also a sense of an invisible presence, something watchful, guarding this abandoned homestead.

We learned that the first Barton to come to this hill had been Gideon, to whom the northern wilderness beckoned after Bunker Hill and the Battle of Bennington. He cleared an acre, put up a log shelter, and went back to Massachusetts to fetch his Betsy, whose waist, it is still told by her descendants, was so slender Gideon's two hands went once around and then halfway round again.

Gideon chose his land on a hillside rather than in the valley where other settlers were beginning to clear their fields. It was cheaper, of course, than fertile riverside acreage, but there is no doubt Gideon was a man who wished to be able to look out from a high point and survey the world while he kept his distance from it. There were winds on the heights, but also sunlight in the hours when the valley might lie in shadow. So he laid out his southfacing fields, erected a lofty 65-foot barn in 1791 with Jude Kent, who came to help from the next hill over, and at the turn of the century, his sons helping to fit the mortise-and-tenon beams and hammering in the hewn pegs and handforged nails, he constructed this house.

Gideon was building for the future. His sons and their sons made their own kingdom here, clearing land in every direction, prying out boulders and making fence, enlarging their herds, killing marauding bears and bobcats, planting gardens and fruit trees, gathering sap from the sugar bush.

By 1860, two young Bartons, Lawrence and Rudyard, could take satisfaction in the farm their forebears had established. But Lawrence went off to die at Gettysburg, and Rud was left to care for his aging parents and manage the farm alone. Rud was a prodigious worker, and ambitious. He planted hop vines on the hillside, and built a drying shed; the hops went to make beer for the Union Army, and Rud put the profits into sheep, selling the wool for uniforms. In the years after the Civil War, farmers all over Vermont were raising sheep. Rud sent to Australia for Merinos to improve his flocks, paying as much as a thousand dollars for a ram. For a time the Barton farm knew unprecedented prosperity. But sheep could be raised more cheaply on the ranges opening up in the West, and Vermonters found it hard to compete. Nevertheless, Rud kept the farm running efficiently. His sense of stewardship never faltered.

Rud's son Timothy had from boyhood done his father's bidding, milking, haying, cleaning out the springs, picking apples, shoveling manure on the fields, taking the ox team to the woods to log. Rud trained his son well, but held the reins too long. He was still undisputed boss of every detail of daily operations until his death in his eighty-fifth year.

Timothy, middle-aged, found independence unsettling. He had no practice in making decisions, and wavered under responsibility. His son Henley remembers his father's frequent trips to the cellar where the cider barrel sat amidst the stored potatoes and cabbages, offering a fermented consolation. "One night I couldn't stand it," Henley recalls. "Pa had been down there three–four times already and was fixing to go again. I slipped down before him and pulled out the bung. He was mad aright, but he never could blame me for it."

The farm, less tightly overseen than it had been under Rud's all-seeing eye, began to lose some of its productivity.

By the time Henley inherited it, he found it hard going. His children were all very young. A mortgage was taken out, and one day, after the grindingly hard times of the thirties, it had to be foreclosed. Eight generations of Bartons had worked this farm. Now it would go to a neighbor who would keep the hayfields open and prop up the barn but who had no time for more.

Then we came — strangers.

We had been looking for a country dwelling for some years. We had a fair idea of what we wanted, and, having had first-hand experience in restoring and living in old Vermont farmhouses, were not unaware of the pitfalls that went with the picturesque. We had heard about the Barton place from our friends the Scotts, who had some years earlier bought the Old Jude Kent place on Birch Hill, just over the way from Barton Hill. We had, in fact, been sitting together in a Moorish village overlooking the Mediterranean, when the Scotts, who had come to inspect the Quaker refugee operation we were carrying on during the Algerian War, first spoke of the old Barton place. "You ought to come and look at it when you get home," they advised us, and as they described it, it did indeed sound interesting, and very far from the cork forests and desert sands of North Africa.

It was several years before we found ourselves on Barton Hill, walking through the high grass, each calling out to the other to look at some new discovery: the brook, the hay loft, the privy, the apple orchard. When at last we entered the house, we fell silent, going quietly through the maze of little rooms, smelling the ingrained odor of all old New England farmhouses, that acerbic bouquet that lingers long after the kerosene lanterns, lye soap, overwintered rutabagas, fried pork and wood smoke have gone.

This day, there were no more ghostly emanations than you'd expect from any venerable uninhabited house.

William's practiced eye took in the structural flaws and dilapidation. We mentally took down partitions and opened more windows to the glorious view. "It's in dreadful shape," we concurred, and went away to think about it.

We agreed that we wanted the kind of privacy the Barton place promised — not another house in sight. Yet we wanted to be not too far from a village, an independent Vermont community, not an adjunct to a ski resort or a college or a second-home development; in the valley, three miles distant from Barton Hill, was a comely village, relatively isolated for long years, which had kept its own self-sufficient character. We needed a house large enough for our six children, for the three already married to come bringing their own. We could not be farmers, yet we wanted to raise our own food and tend as we could to the needs of neglected land.

We came back to look, several times. The children were enthusiastic. William's lawyer brother pronounced it a beautiful piece of land but the house fit only for demolition. But William, as an architect, could envision a restoration to the comfort and welcome the house had once offered.

One day William stood in the center of what had once been the parlor and applied a crowbar to the cracked plaster of the ceiling. He wanted to see what kind of beams might be under the plaster, a reasonable enough precaution. But at the touch of the crowbar a heavy jagged section of the ceiling fell directly on his head, striking his temple, slashing through his mouth. "Good Lord," he managed to say through the streams of blood, "I've never been attacked by a house before. It doesn't seem to want us here."

We drove fifteen miles to a doctor, who sewed up William's lip and bandaged his eye. We returned, chastened.

"I don't believe it's because the house doesn't want us," I ventured, to my own surprise. "It's because they want to be sure we're serious about it."

"*They?*"

"Yes. The Bartons. It's still their house. You must have felt them watching while we've been poking around."

"But you don't believe in ghosts!"

"No. Well, they're not exactly ghosts, not spooks in white sheets. More of a presence, just beyond our vision. They loved this house. They'd rather see it continue falling gently into decay than have the wrong family fixing it up and thinking it's all theirs."

"I see. And this crack on the head is a kind of test?"

"Exactly."

"Well," said William ruefully, "I suppose that's fair enough. I just hope it doesn't take more than one such test. We are serious, aren't we?"

"Yes," I said. "I think we are."

In the end, we bought the Barton place. For two years we came at intervals, bringing measuring tape and notebook. We slept in the hay loft of the sheep barn, and cooked on a campfire made of a circle of fieldstones. We began to know the place in varying seasons, and to learn something of the weathers on the hill. We made and remade plans for the house.

At last we were ready for the task of rebuilding It was a tremendous undertaking. It took over a year, with the amiable village contractor and his fine crew of carpenters working along with William. The whole house was lifted on jacks to excavate a basement and construct new foundations. The woodshed was forwarded the few feet it needed to be in alignment with the house, and joined with a passageway. Four chimneys were built. A well was drilled, a septic tank installed. Plumbing and wiring went in, a wood-burning furnace and an oil burner. The old beams with their axe marks were exposed, their massive lengths cleaned and polished. The rickety stairways were replaced. Where the wide pine floor boards were usable, they were sanded and stained. The metal roof was repaired and painted black. Insulation went into the walls. New windows were added. New shutters were painted dark green, the clapboards white.

Now the house looked fresh and inviting, but not like a new house. With all the repairs and changes, it still kept its original lines and its integrity had not been violated.

We moved in, though much remained to be done, in August. Because my father was dying that summer, I had to be away when some of the unpacking and settling was done, but the children, big and little, opened crates, put books on shelves, and helped William arrange the furniture. By September there was some order, and even times of quiet in the house.

Then I began to be aware that the Bartons had not left. It was not just that with my father's death I was more than usually sensitive to the passage of generations. Nor was it simply that the sounds an old house makes with the approach of winter can often seem either ghostly or disturbingly human. We could dismiss the sudden hysterical midnight barking of our collie, Joy, as simply her reaction to the crossing of deer or woodchucks over the line she had marked around the house to define her territory, even though she could not see the intruders from her pantry sleeping-place.

It was something else, something palpable which I felt very strongly that first year. It was particularly powerful in the wing of the house, and especially in one bedroom, where, we learned later, an old blind grandmother had spent many years in what must have been a sorrowful darkness. But it was also present elsewhere. It was not menacing ectoplasm lurking behind doors to leap out with horrid shriek. I never *saw* anything at all. It was rather that sometimes in the shadows beyond the hearth where we sat reading quietly of an evening, I would feel someone standing, watching, judging — old Rudyard, perhaps, disapproving an extravagant use of firewood. Or I would look out the south window and be certain that Betsy or Millie or one of the other wives was beside me, thinking to herself, "Those are *our* hills." In one tiny bedroom, when it was quite empty, I could almost hear the sound of the breathing of a sleeping child.

I was not quite frightened, but I confess it made me uneasy. I really do not believe in ghosts and apparitions. I am generally rational. Yet there it was. There was no denying this sense of a kind of shadowy life parallel to ours. I spoke about it to no one, even William, though he and I would joke from time to time when from our bedroom an unexplained sound very like footsteps could be heard in the living room below: "That must be old Gideon going out to check on the cows in the barn this wicked cold night," or "Could that be Timothy on his way to the cider barrel?"

We loved the house. I was happier here than I had ever been anywhere, and more so each day. As time went on, I began to feel that the Bartons knew this, that as they became less concerned about our alien presence, the weight of their own presence lessened. The disconcerting sounds in the night were fewer. When summer came, they seemed to have gone out into the sunlight and the westerly breezes. With autumn, they came inside once more, but so quietly they hardly fanned the air. That second winter, I knew them to be still there, but contentedly so, resting, dreaming themselves back into the past, no longer so troubled about the present, no longer agitated by the new family within their walls.

It has been fifteen years now, and they scarcely ever make themselves known in that unmistakable way any longer.

It is still their house, and always will be.

Now it is also ours.

If the day is fair, hay is put not in the mangers where it has gone all winter, but scattered out in the barnyard on the thawed ground. The horses welcome this as a change and a treat, biting and chomping with a jaunty air, thrusting and bobbing their heads. Their coats are so luxuriously plush, so handsomely colored in tones of mahogany and chestnut, that it puts once more the question of why nature so frequently arranges shapes and colors and textures of such delight to the human eye.

Everything in nature, even its waste, is functional, but rarely are its forms exclusively utilitarian. There is a gloriously extravagant hand at work, shaping and painting, molding, framing and lighting, putting into motion and endowing with grace, with an endless ingenuity and incomparable skill, and to what end? Some of this glory is clearly part of the pattern of ongoing creation — bird plumage, butterfly wings, the arrangement of stamens, pistils, petals. But a non-reproductive rock does not have to be so nobly sculptured, so rich with facets and veins of mineral-shine. A snowflake does not have to be so intricately, uniquely elegant in its hexagonal composition. A sky does not have to arrange itself into a sunset so opulent it takes the breath away.

It would seem that all these marvels of design are observed and responded to chiefly by humans. Does a dog (even one as intelligent as our collies Joy and Mr. MacGregor) sit quietly in awe of a sunset, a bird gasp at the sight of a barley field rippling in the wind, a frog pause in his croaking to rejoice in the pattern made by a patch of reeds reflected in the glistening surface of the pond? One cannot be arbitrary about it, but it would appear that they do not. But — can all this prodigal beauty be simply a gift for our human eyes?

It seems presumptuous to think so — it was all there before Adam, and, unless in our folly we destroy it utterly, it will still go on after the last of the race disappears. Perhaps there was implanted within us a reaction to the artistry of nature so that we, with our capacity for destruction, would stay our hands, and our capacity for loving and tending would be roused in its stead. Man's response to natural beauty could be the sole factor guarding against total exploitation and ravaging of the earth. Perhaps a miraculous interworking of retina and brain will make the message so clear — *the beauty of this earth is unique, irreplaceable, and we are the custodians of that beauty* — that this will be the salvation of the world from our greed and aggression.

That steward is best who loves what he cares for, and we, loving the earth for its beauty, may yet know ourselves its stewards.

One of the pleasant things about Town Meeting Day is the noon recess when everyone gathers in the church hall for the meal served by the Ladies Alliance. There are platters of meat loaf, a variety of baked beans, mounds of potato salad, stacks of homemade bread and rolls, shimmering rings of fruit-studded gelatine, slabs of apple, cherry, pumpkin, custard and blueberry pie, as well as devil's food and angel cake, all served up with good hot coffee. In addition to this gastronomic plenty, there is the opportunity to visit with the fellow-townspeople who share your table, with some of whom you may not have exchanged more than a word or two since last year's meeting. And whatever the differences of opinion concerning the articles on the Warning, the noonday dinner is a time of congeniality.

At our table this year, the talk turned to energy, the solar house being built above the Morrow place, the controversy over a proposed hydroelectric dam on the Black River, the way wood smoke rises straight up from everybody's chimneys throughout the valley on a still frosty morning, and the success of the company making cast iron stoves in the next town over. Someone mentioned the fluctuating price of fuel oil and another recalled the gas shortage of a few years ago. Philo Ward, who presides over the local filling station, was not convinced that petroleum is an inexhaustible resource. "You could be driving up to the pump one of these days again, sooner than maybe you'd think, and I'd just be giving you two–three gallons, if you're lucky, to last you a week or more."

The possible return of gas rationing interested everyone at the table, in particular young Theodore, son of one of the old farming families. Theodore wears his hair in a pony tail and supports a dense beard. He lives with his girl in a cabin at the edge of his father's property, and works hard keeping the old place going, sugaring, planting, harvesting, logging. Theodore has a 1967 Dodge he hadn't finished repairing before snow fell, so he's done a lot of walking this winter. He has been thinking about the price of gasoline for some time, and studying the alternatives.

"Fellow out in California has it beat," says Theodore. "He's making methane gas out of chicken manure, and he's running all his farm machinery on it." Helping himself to a second, different, slice of pie, he adds thoughtfully, "I might be getting myself some chickens."

The discussion that followed brought out some well-honed curiosity and speculation on the particulars of methane production. Philo had the final word on chicken manure as fuel for private transportation: "If you want my opinion, it sure would cut down on tailgating."

It was a satisfactory discussion, ending on just the right note. It didn't matter that everyone present understood that methane gas is actually odorless. Philo had simply rounded things off with the kind of traditional remark that keeps large matters in sharp local focus.

In most town meetings there will be discussion of questions of importance, some of them hotly controversial — the school budget, a new grader for the town road crew, fluoridation, property taxes, zoning, the nuclear freeze resolution, funds for the day care center. But no matter how grave or heated the deliberations, nearly always someone will rise and with a canny, waggish sentence or two restore perspective and good humour.

It may not have been just this that Calvin Coolidge had in mind when in a rare moment of eloquence he said, "There is something in every town meeting, in every election, that approaches very near to the sublime." Vermonters know what Coolidge meant, and by and large they would agree. But they would also know that such sublimity would never be total, would always be limited by the humanity of the participants, and by a wry recognition of the persistence, in all our affairs, of the element of the ridiculous.

One of the retired federal officials who has bought a house in the development uphill was heard to pronounce the Town Meeting obsolete. It's archaic and inefficient, he says.

Maybe.

But if he lives here long enough, he may come around to seeing why it is cherished by the people of this village and region as the best form of local government yet devised. Not quite sublime, but the best so far.

We have had our St. Patrick's day blizzard, followed by rain, followed by brief idyllic interval of balm and sun, followed by plunging temperatures and freeze-up, followed by tentative thaws, followed by sleet — a whole extravagant orchestration of weather playing every theme in the repertoire of March.

Back roads are predictably gouged into muddy chaos, paved roads potholed and humped to a degree that can make a downhill ride alarming as a descent on a crude roller coaster. Warning signs make their annual appearance, stark black letters on red squares: FROST HEAVES, and sometimes, a little farther along, simply BUMP. Everyone drives cautiously, slowly, during this interval, but even so, accidents happen. Young Spruce Patterson was taken to the hospital last week when his Jeep flipped over. He has injured his spine, and must lie quietly in pain for several weeks, brooding over the job he had been hired to start the day of the accident, logging over on Bethlehem Hill.

Over at the Miller place, the stretch of road by their house is so tortuously rutted, mud so treacherous and deep, that it is impassable. George Miller drives his pick-up truck as near as he can get, then gets out and walks the rest of the way home. "Got to have it," he says philosophically. "Got to get the frost out of the ground. And nobody's figured yet a better way to do it."

But it is a time of inconvenience, a time when everything looks drab, coated, crusted and awash, a time of impatient waiting for the splendid next act for which this is such a tiresome prologue. One almost feels frost-heaves within the soul, the great upward thrust of winter's doomed authority pushing, distorting, cracking the frozen layers of one's being, going through the yearly dislodgement, the necessary expulsion of every last particle of ice from the ground of the spirit, to prepare for the entry of spring.

"God was so clever," says little Emma, "making all those animals —

teeth and fur and all that complicated stuff. Of course," she added after a moment's thought, "it took Him a whole day."

There is never a walk without some reward, however small. This day is a bright March jewel, the sky glistening blue, the sun warm on old snow. We expected turbulent weather today — the radio issued a storm warning last night, predicting a major blizzard moving out of the west, telling us of heavy snowfalls in the Ohio valley and the Alleghanies. But the storm has passed far to the south, leaving this portion of the map to cloudless skies and a temperature perfectly combining crispness and warmth.

I am glad for the handsome day. Still, as I walk the familiar uphill road and take the fork westward, looking for something, anything, of note in the bright landscape, I see nothing new, no signs of early spring growth beyond what I'd observed a day or two ago. I am never insensible of my enormous undeserved good fortune to be living in this place, I find it beautiful in every season, but this day I am momentarily bored by the sameness of the scene.

Mr. MacGregor is not in the least bored. He always races outside in the expectation of hundreds of new fascinations to be discovered in field and roadside, and he is never disappointed. Today I envy a bit this unfailing enthusiasm, the joy he takes in every odor and track. He will pause for moments sniffing a perfectly banal-looking heap of snow, evidently hearing and smelling all kinds of excitements beneath its surface — voles, mice, or chipmunks perhaps. There is obvious pleasure in lifting the leg and leaving a saffron flower in the snow at each such stopping-place, and there is sheer happiness in his eyes as he gallops to catch up with me. He couldn't possibly imagine a human disinterest in this entrancing countryside.

So I ramble along, contented enough, really, but deciding that this time there will not be anything particularly memorable to carry home in my thoughts, as one brings back a bit of moss, a shell, a handful of wildflowers from such excursions.

But I am mistaken, as I ought to have known I'd be. I do see something I have not seen before, and it is a surprise. Quite some distance from the house by way of the road, though perhaps only a quarter-mile as thistledown flies, I see amongst a clump of small bare-limbed poplars and alders two willows, tall and quite slender, all decked with enormous silvery buds. They are not at all like the miniature tight buds that appear on the scraggly wild willows that spring up everywhere in moist patches. These are fat, glossy, luxuriant, even extravagant in their velvet elegance, neatly placed on well-formed branches. And I understand in a flash that these are no wildings. They are the same pussy willows sold on the streets of Paris in the grey season after Christmas, bred for grace and plushness. They are offspring of the cultivated French pussywillows we planted near our house fourteen years ago.

Those fragile sticks we put in the ground along our stone wall have risen to heights of thirty feet or more, thriving in the sheltered space where the soil seems damp even in midsummer, and each year giving us more and more largesse of those appealing furry aments. In one of those years, after the grey velvet turned to golden-green blossom, a northeasterly breeze silently wafted seed over the hayfields and copses to find their resting place here on the hillside. They took root and shot up alongside the young poplars and alders without anyone noticing. Now they are established and can announce themselves with confidence.

How debonair they are, softly shining in the afternoon sunlight! They almost purr with satisfaction at having pioneered so success-fully, children making good on their own, far from home.

Andrew, winging in from several months in California, looks around our March landscape and pronounces it "pretty bleak." He tells us about the sunlit gardens and balmy temperatures that make a per-petual summer in that Pacific country. I look at our drab hills and the fields still raggedly cloaked in snow, and have to admit, that, for the moment, it is *triste*.

Later that day I ascend the sheep trail, the footing uncertain over patches of old snow and last year's matted brown grass slippery with mud and ice. Deer have been here — there are hoof-prints and fresh droppings. An owl has lost a feather, a little plume, really, delicately fluffed along the quill, in shades of ash tipped with silver. Rivulets of ice-cold meltwater are making their way downward, enlarging their channels and joining forces to create a sizable pond in a semicircle of spruce that has grown up in the field below. The little streams are quick and tuneful, and clear as glass. When you stoop to examine them, they reveal a whole microcosm of new growth. Bright green and small as baby's fingernails, leaves of budding cress and marsh marigolds grow in whorls and garlands under the rushing water. They are infinitesimal now, but the promise is there of great adornments, emerald and gold, where now there seems nought but weary snow and homely mud. I go home reassured that spring is making its preliminary advances. It *will* come.

As a minor salute to St. Patrick, I held the last of last year's potatoes for an Irish dinner on the seventeenth. Of course they are Kennebecs, good keepers in the root cellar, and not Killarney tubers, but it is all the same in the stomach. These along with a rich stew swimming in gravy, and for dessert something my ethnic cookbook calls "Maggie Murphy's Aunt's Coffeecake," made for a family celebration, though the ancestral trees seem to contain only Anglo-Irish.

Saint Patrick was a Briton, anyway, and only got to Ireland because he was captured by Irish raiders and transported there into slavery, where for years he shepherded his master's flocks "in the woods and on the mountain...in snow, frost and rain." He couldn't stay away, though, once he escaped back to England, for he kept hearing in his dreams "the voice of the Irish" calling him back. There's a legend that tells of Patrick living during the forty days of Lent in the year 441 in a hut on a mountain in County Mayo. "Fighting manfully against the temptations of demons," he was attacked by a witch who threw garlic water at him to kill him as part of a spell, but the saint nimbly hurled back his missionary's handbell and slew her on the spot.

Needless to say, I did not put garlic water in our stew.

Redpolls — a flock of 60 or 70 — come now to the birdseed scattered on the rotting snow. Their movements in unison are a sociable choreography in these grey, still days. How they rise together in an instant, wheeling upward into the bare architecture of the maples, then arcing beyond them to alight in a venerable apple tree, resting there only a moment before raining down again upon the circle of seed! The invisible discipline that shapes these linked flights is a feathered mystery, part of the eternal charm of birds.

On the west slope of the hill today, along the ridge road where an occasional fragment of blue sky was reflected in mudpuddles, the weary snow lay in untidy heaps. Beyond the culvert draining a rambunctious force of icy water, a mound of soiled snow no different from the rest — but resting on it a triad of snow buntings. What delicate little beings they look, but hardy, of course, beyond most of their fellows. When they flew upward and off, it was in the most exquisite patterns, as if they were flying to the measures of a trio for flutes.

It has been the year of the mouse. The county agent informs us that it goes in cycles, and this has been the year they multiply like lemmings. Damage has been extensive. Of the semi-dwarf apple trees, grape vines and raspberries we planted last year, little survives. It is hard not to curse at the sight of girdled trunks and stems, nibbled winter-long under the snow cover and now coming to light. The elderberry bushes that grew so prodigally within the base of the vanished silo were gnawed almost to extinction. What a feast those rodents enjoyed, all cozy and protected beneath their winter blanket!

I give the cats full leave to aid in restoring the balance of nature.

The vapors rising from the rifts in the river ice suggest steam pluming from a thousand teakettles, or hot Mephistophelean clouds from a subterranean inferno. But their heat is only a few degrees above that of the freezing air that furnishes this brilliant day. The condensation produces that recurrent wonder of hoar frost riming every twig and branch of the trees and shrubs that fringe the river bank, and the eye is pleasured by the sinuous silver columns of bloom patterning the white reaches of snowfields beneath a cobalt sky. It is a scene from a northern fairy tale, a landscape in which at any moment a jeweled sleigh will appear, drawn by silver-grey horses whose flared nostrils emit puffs of white in perfect roundlets, while within her ermine swathings the single passenger sits in imperial stillness, her

15

eyes glittering like diamonds — the Ice Princess, journeying to her palace of snow.

Helen Lincoln laughed when she told me about going to see her friend Sarah Pease the other day. Helen was exhausted from caring for her ailing husband; Sarah too was overfatigued. They sat in the parlor and had spoken only a few words about their respective concerns and responsibilities of family, farm, and community when they both dropped off to sleep. They woke simultaneously an hour later to say to each other as they parted, "Now wasn't that a nice visit?"

On a moist afternoon near twilight, the ground underfoot mud-snow-ice, the fields dull white, the hills indigo, the sky a dense grey, there is a stillness in the air as I walk along, in what seems a not unpleasant vacuum. But as soon as I stop, stand quiet with boots no longer thudding and ears open to sounds not of my own making, the air begins to vibrate. I am conscious now of a chain-saw, far off but importunate in its whine — someone is logging over beyond the spruce-filled hollow. Then overhead a straggle of crows flaps its way west with that strident cawing which we find not unwelcome in these days before the spring birds return with fairer harmonies. Their passage is an untidy scrawl against the sky, a harsh but exurberant clamoring. Once gone, there is silence for a space, then over by the sleeping apple trees comes a thin brief trill which is the solitary plaint of the red squirrel whose mate we trapped and deported a day or so ago. When this is heard no more, there comes a sudden staccato hammering. That is a woodpecker, I think, with a sudden lift of spirit. I haven't heard his tireless vibrato here for months, I'd forgotten how cheering it could be with its message of bird-at-work.

The deathly quiet of midwinter is at last succeeded by a tentative overture to spring. Had I not stood in silence for those moments, I might have missed it.

On the Saturday afternoon before Easter, snow begins to fall, and the muddy bare patches, with their hint of green to come, are once again covered with white. Easter morning dawns grey, with only a touch of rose-pearl in the east.

It is 5:45 a.m. Jeeps and station wagons climb the mountain road to North Hollow and stop at the broad meadow below the old square Talbot farmhouse. The new snow overlaid on the remaining winter drifts makes it too deep to venture far into the field. We stand, some thirty of us, in our Easter finery — parkas, ski pants, woolen caps and mittens. A cock crows from the direction of the Mitchell farm farther up the hollow.

"Alleluia, alleluia, dance with the Lord!" we sing, hopping from one foot to another, our voices thin in the Christmas-card landscape.

The pastor reads the ancient words: "As it began to dawn toward the first day of the week, came Mary Magdalene and the other Mary to see the sepulchre...the angel of the Lord descended from Heaven and rolled back the stone...his countenance was like lightning and his raiment white as snow...Fear not ye, He is not here; for he is risen..."

We walk together a little distance up the hill as the pastor continues reading. "And behold, two of them went that same day to a village called Emmaus...and while they communed together and reasoned, Jesus himself drew near, and went with them. But their eyes were holden that they should not know him...Then he said unto them, O fools, and slow of heart to believe...They constrained him, saying, Abide with us...And he went in to tarry with them. And it came to pass, as he sat at meat with them, he took bread, and blessed it, and brake, and gave to them. And their eyes were opened, and they knew him..."

Again we sing "Alleluia!" and form a circle. The pastor takes from the hand of the shy retired school teacher, she whose voice had risen clear and sweet above the rest in our singing, the two wheat loaves she had baked the day before.

He holds the loaves quietly for a moment before speaking. "Now, after this three days' fasting which has given us a small recognition of what hunger is to millions in this world, and in remembrance of all victims of war whether called enemy or friend, all who hunger or are in sorrow or in need, as our Lord taught us, we break this bread and share it." In silence, each one tears a piece from the loaf and passes it, smiling, to his neighbor.

The birds, whose calendar has told them it is spring whatever the weather, have come north to us again, and their music is everywhere — blackbird, robin, killdeer, junco, kingfisher, and, in the distance, the rhythmic notes of the woodpecker's pounding, faintly recalling the strokes of hammer on nails at Calvary.

Someone quietly points out that the shifting of the strengthening light has illuminated the gable of the capacious old grey barn across the road, revealing a design cut into the wood long ago, small circles arranged in the shape of a cross.

The service is over. We move back toward our cars, toddlers riding in their fathers' arms, and greet one another cheerfully. Down the hill we go, to the village where breakfast prepared by the men of the Lions Club awaits us in the school cafeteria: pancakes, dressed in sweet dairy butter and the Mitchells' maple syrup, accompanied by crisp sausages and mugs of steaming coffee.

The valley warms as rents in the leaden sky reveal fields of blue.

By eleven o'clock, when the doors of the white churches receive their congregations for the formal Easter services, the street is running silver with melted snow, and the sun is triumphant overhead.

Alleluia!

Now I am into my basement gardening in all seriousness. Eight long tubes suspended over tables radiate an unearthly glow. Beneath them, peat pots and seed flats filled with a growing mixture and spagnum moss hold a multitude of seeds. Planted so far: broccoli, brussels sprouts, cabbage, cauliflower, cantaloup, eggplant, green peppers, celery, and, direct result of the seductions of the seed catalogues, seven kinds of tomatoes. It is cool down in the basement, the snow blanks out the high windows, and the light is artificial, yet nothing can change the elemental feel of the act of putting seed in soil.

At 8:30 this morning, the gamewarden's car eases into a rutted siding below our pond, and he gets out to look around. I stop on the way to the village.

"Anything wrong?"

"Nope, but could be."

It seems there is a pack of dogs loose on the other side of the hill, headed this way, presumably chasing deer. (I thank God Mr. Mac-Gregor is safely attached to his trolley-line between maple and apple tree. His shepherding instincts can be roused by the undisciplined rompings of deer on his property.)

"It's about the worst of times for deer, and those dogs know it."

"Whose dogs are they?"

"Come from that place down by Kelly's where they let 'em run free. People don't realize. I had a pair of dogs yesterday, caught them right in the woods. Belonged to a couple of fellows from New Jersey. Said they had to keep the dogs locked up in the city all the time, they were just giving them a holiday, letting them off the leash in Vermont. I had to explain to them why it wasn't a good idea."

"What did you do with the dogs?"

"Tied them up and waited until the guys came looking for them. Told them I'd have to shoot their pets next time." The warden shakes his head. "I sure would hate to be a nine months pregnant doe coming down to browse and have to outrun a dog with snow this deep still in the woods."

I leave him there, on guard, squinting down the southeast slope where somewhere in the woods danger roves to threaten the herd he is sworn to protect. A good man, and a patient man. I am glad he is there.

On Easter Sunday, appropriately, a dove arrived at the bird feeder. It was clearly exhausted, huddling on the ground, picking up scattered seed with erratic movements of its shapely head. It fluttered to the lowest bough of the maple tree and rested for a long time.

On Easter Monday, the dove seemed less fatigued, feeding quietly amongst the lively blue jays, juncos and blackbirds. It seemed not to notice the other birds at all, surrounding itself with a bubble of solitude.

On Tuesday morning when we looked out, there were two doves on the maple bough. The newcomer was larger, rosy-breasted, no doubt the male of a conjugal pair. They fed together at intervals, flying in tandem back to their perch.

In the days since, they have been nowhere visible. I have looked anxiously and frequently, but there is no sign of the doves. Perhaps they have flown down Barton Hill to the halfway point where in other years a pair has often been seen taking dust-baths in the road and weaving in and out of the overhanging branches. The same pair? I hope so. I hope it is a loving couple reunited and returned to their summer haven, there to start once more the first of several broods of the season in safety and peace.

Snow began falling last night. This morning, it was winter once more. It snowed all day long, more than twenty inches of snow, piling up in theatrical drifts. William was back on his tractor, ploughing us out again. I shoveled a narrow path to the front door. (A north-facing front door is not really advisable in this subArctic zone.) The snow was exceedingly heavy and wet, packing down grimly under the advance of shovel and plough.

Daffodils and tulips which had ventured upwards in the interval between the last storm and this are invisible now. How high is the temperature under the snow blanket? Not summery, surely, but warm enough, I pray, to protect these foolhardy reconaissance troops.

There is no more birdfeed at the market; everyone has responded to broadcast appeals to keep the birds, especially the migrants, nourished in this untimely replay of January. We put out bread crumbs, suet, raisins, and little pots of peanut butter. What could we raise, I wonder — besides sunflowers and thistles — that would suit the birds and provide an inexpensive supply that would last not just through the winter months but also April's follies?

The cold is inexorable, freezing the masses of snow in place. Occasional flurries add new laminations. The road to the Wilsons' house last night was a scene from Dr. Zhivago. Spruces were so heavily laden with snow their branches angled until they assumed cypress shapes. Birches arced like acrobats. Every twig of every tree, bush, and bramble bent under a weight of white, and burdened branches scraped at the car as we passed along the narrowed road into vistas of silver. One felt oneself inside a window-pane picture etched by frost.

Today, brief sunshine at intervals, the brook racing and roaring and proclaiming its rebellion against winter's prolonged grasp. A host of birds dispute their claims at the outdoor larder we have prepared for them — grosbeaks, field sparrows, purple finches. Mr. MacGregor gobbled up all their suet-and-peanut-butter, then threw up all over the Persian carpet.

Spring is in a holding pattern over Vermont.

But down in the basement the broccoli, bless its eager heart, is sprouting boldly under the false sunlight.

Brussels sprouts, cabbage and cauliflower seedlings catching up with broccoli, showing their true leaves, a healthy blue-green color.

Temperatures so far this month are eight degrees below average. I fear I shall lose my wager (a trillion dollars) with William that the boulder he moved out on the pond ice will have sunk into water during the third week in April. This boulder, transported with enormous difficulty by bulldozer from the vegetable garden to the pond during January, is meant to sink gently downward as the ice melts and form a diving platform at the edge of the water. It is sitting there now in frozen solitude, impossible to envision as an element in sunlit swimming parties in July.

How could I have been so optimistic last month as to make a bet that the ice would be all out and the boulder sunk in place so early in the season? Katie was more cautious — she placed her bet on the fourth week in April, and William, with exemplary prudence, chose the second week in May. He tells me with false pity, "I'm sorry about that trillion dollars you're going to be losing." I brazen it out and assure him he is the one who will be paying me.

But that pond ice looks as if it will be there forever, and the boulder locked in place till Kingdom Come.

A bawdy south wind has blown in, teasing the temperature upward and reducing the icicles to tears. This morning I saw the first robin flying over the horse fence at Appletree Farm.

No more room on the basement tables, so the guest bathroom has been taken over for trays of peat pots planted with petunias, pansies, forget-me-nots, ageratum, snapdragons, and marigolds.

Yesterday the river was dazzling, suggesting a swiftly moving mass of silver fish reflecting the intense sunlight. Today, under dull skies, it is a hard green, hastening roughly along with hints of baleful purpose, pressing outward over the banks, snarling "Out of my way! Out of my way!"

Thomas Hunter's meadow, tended and enriched for generations, one of the great beauties of the riverside south of the village, was ravaged by ice floes last week. A whole section was entirely washed away; an 8-foot gully splits another portion; the drainage ditches are silted up.

"Can the damage be repaired?" Thomas was asked.

"Some," he replied. "But they say it takes a million years to build up an inch of topsoil. Guess I won't be around to see what I lost put back."

At breakfast this morning, another sign of spring: a svelte weasel streaking back and forth by the stone wall, his winter coat turned to a velvety brown except for a handsome white patch on his chest. He showed up strikingly against the snow but moved so swiftly the eye could scarcely follow his graceful spirals. He darted in and out of the stones and tangled vines for several minutes, perhaps hunting an invisible chipmunk. At moments he seemed simply to be playing, bounding high and running in circles in sheer enjoyment of the mild air. He may have been following by ear the movements of voles under the snow. Several starlings swooped into the ash tree and began shrieking obscenities at the weasel, who appeared to ignore them. But the next moment he was gone, not to reappear. Somehow I feel that this was a one-time performance, that we shall not, simply looking out the window, see him again.

Rivulets are eroding the snowfields, the patches of dull matted grass widen. If you look closely, you can see an infinity of little folded blades, pale green, grass in the fetal stage, which will soon be stretching upward to give the landscape a new and welcome color. At the end of the lane, guarding Joy's grave, the old cottonwood tree, my dear misshapen valiant favorite, has survived another winter of violent west winds and is looking almost girlish in a gauze of palest silver-olive, that color the ancients thought to be the hue of Athena's eyes. Brambles and osiers are carmine as if blood were pulsing through their limbs, the willows have taken on a bold amber tint, the maples are rosier every day. All those tiny swelling buds have given our world a softer contour and tinge. The stark sculpture of the mountains is overlaid by a perceptible haze, the black-and-white which has defined our view for months now warms into delicate washes of rusty-pink. At sunset, the oblique rays intensify these shy tints into the most radiant swaths of coral and mauve. And it is all done by a tumescent leaf bud, no bigger than a chipmunk's ear, multiplied by billions.

It was a poor season for sugaring, but we had first-run syrup — delectable — on ice cream at my mother's house last night, she having been the lucky recipient of a gift of half a pint from the neighbor's boy who is tapping the maples in her yard.

Molly and the boys spied both a quick red fox making for the deer yard and a fat woodchuck taking the air beside his burrow in the upper mowing. After a relatively unpopulated landscape for a long white season, it is heartening to see the neighbors who were there all the time.

The rain slacks off late in the afternoon, and the descending sun gleams through racks of cloud on a sudden gathering of mist in the valley. Swirling, rising and falling, catching the amber light, the vaporous forms shift and dance. Up on our hill the sky clears in time for the first stars, but driving downward to the village, one is quickly surrounded by fog again, pressing with soft implacability against windshield and headlights.

The village is ghostly, streetlights haloed, lamplit windows blurred squares, the common veiled, silent and dripping. The fog seems to creep into the library room where a faithful little group, dedicated to preserving the town history, is met to talk of a summer exhibition of local artifacts. Our voices are muted, the lights dimmer than usual, the discussion desultory.

Suddenly the hideous giant-scream of the fire siren shatters the night. It wails and vibrates, slides to a moan, pauses, howls, again and again. We sit transfixed, every face stricken. Every heart is stopped by the question, Is it *my* house?

The youngest male present dashes out the door, and the oldest female reaches for the telephone to ask "Where is it?" The rest of us rise and peer out the library door while one automobile after another speeds up the main street through the fog, bearing volunteers to the fire station.

In a gratifyingly short time, the fire engines roar to life, clanging and ablaze with scarlet lights blurring in the fog. They halt on the far side of the common, and though they are scarcely visible from the library door, we can hear the hoarse voices shouting orders and the sounds of ladders being elevated and hoses gushing.

"It's the Cochran place."

We stand and shiver, not so much from damp and cold as in knowing that spacious old wooden house has been made over into apartments, now inhabited by several families.

It is hardly possible to be sure through the murk, but there seem to be no flames shooting out of windows or roof. Perhaps it is only a small interior fire, already under control.

Someone makes a small joke: "Probably just boiling sap in the kitchen, and it boiled over."

Recognizing that we cannot be helpful, we return to our circle of chairs and continue our deliberations, with one of our number stationed at the door to report at intervals. We finish up our business briskly, and adjourn into the night. The fire engines are still there, but there are no flames to be seen, no shouts of panic, no ambulance screeching off with victims. Clearly it is minor, not a conflagration, and it is taken care of. We go our ways, relieved.

But I discover myself bone-chilled and shaken, creeping back uphill through the spectral night, and overwhelmed with a rush of thankfulness to see our house, in the clear air of the hilltop, windows cheerfully ashine. Not the smouldering black ruin which has been in the forefront of my imagination ever since the first cry of the siren.

This fear of fire is something every country dweller lives with. Local history is so filled with accounts of disaster by fire that no one can be easy on this score for a moment. Twenty miles away in the village where my ancestors lived, their houses marked on the old maps are all gone, all burnt to the ground. This is why we go back after we've started out on a journey, checking to be sure the stove is really off; why we never leave a room without placing a screen before the open fireplace; why we have the chimney-sweep come regularly, and keep matches on a high shelf, and place candles carefully. Yet we know how easily it could all be for nought in an instant's flaring, and this beloved house, so much more to us than mere shelter, could vanish.

Two days later, in the sunlight of a primavera morning, I see Roy and Florence pushing a pram by the common. The baby lies sleeping under a crocheted blanket. He is two months old, and shines all golden in a wooly yellow suit, his hands curled unmittened in that innocence which is meant by nature to touch the heart.

"Roy was out that night," Florence says. She has a pale neo-Raphaelite face and speaks calmly. "I was in the living room, and I heard the flames *crackling*. I ran, just flew, to the baby's room and picked him up and got out to telephone downstairs."

"It's not so bad," Roy says. "Our bedroom got the most of the damage. We lost our clothes, mostly. It didn't spread to the other apartments. They came so quick, and put it out in five minutes."

"How did it start?"

"We don't know." They look at each other and fall silent. Could it have been a cigarette? I do not ask. They do not want to talk about it.

"The baby's all right," Roy says, his face showing more emotion than I'd ever seen him reveal in a community where expressionless features and understatement are the marks of manhood.

"It didn't bother the baby at all," says Florence. "He didn't really wake up at all."

They smile down at this child who will grow up hearing how his mother saved him from the fire on a night the fog was thick as cotton, when he was two months old.

Everywhere the ground has been tunneled by the ubiquitous voles, who heave up squiggles of muddy earth in their endless engineering. Their efforts doubtless contribute to the curious odor in the air these early spring days, an annual phenomenon that lasts about a week. It is a most distinctive scent, a blend of wet subsoil churned to the surface, old rotting vegetation steaming in the sun, run-off from the barn tainting the ephemeral streams that trickle to fields below. It is powerful, but not really unpleasant. It is oddly like the pervasive year-round smell of the Moorish village where we once lived, except for the absence of a particular spice, cumin, indigenous to the Tunisian scene. Here the primal reek will diminish and disappear as the grass burgeons and takes over, soon to bring its own fresh and uncomplicated fragrance.

A fickle day, alternating heavy clouds and slanting sunshine, in midafternoon a surprisingly fierce southwest wind so impetuous it lifted the pine boughs, which had all winter protected the perennial beds, and carried some of them off to the orchard. Then a real April shower, pelting against the windowpanes — what a welcome sound, the first precipitation in months that was not snow or sleet.

William used the snowplow to clean out the stable, long blocked by drifts. Now a heaping treasure of manure awaits expenditure on the vegetable garden. I am reminded that the ancient Romans, who thought of everything in the line of divinities, even had a god in charge of manuring fields. Stercutius was his name. He wasn't one of the glamorous gods boasting giant marble statues and many-columned temples; in fact, he was really the old grandfather god Saturn in one of his workaday roles. But he must have had a lot of prayers to answer as farmers set about their immemorial tasks of enriching their fields and vineyards. To think about Stercutius today makes our manure pile seem one in a noble historic line, to be blessed as it is spread on the waiting garden patch.

While he was at it, William climbed up to open the gable windows in the barn in anticipation of the swallows' arrival around the first of May. Great consternation when he discovered that with the dwindling of the winter's supply of hay which had in effect been supporting it, the whole west end of the barn was on the verge of caving in. Some emergency shoring-up has averted collapse for the time being, but we must face the fact that, yes, the barn needs major repairs.

An utterly capricious day, with chill winds harrying the leaves I tried to rake, cold spitting rain, moments of tepid sunshine, and bad-tempered flurries of real snow. Nevertheless, we worked away for five or six hours, William on his caterpillar tractor, I with rake and spade. The deep mud of the driveway and vegetable garden area compounded our labors. We combined to accomplish the annual task of removing the heavy wide wooden ramp which spends the winter as a walkway between front door and driveway. William raised it on his forklift, I rode on it in an attempt to keep it balanced, managing one spectacular fall in the muddiest mud. But we made it to the barn fence, where the ramp was unloaded under the inquisitive gaze of the horses, Gallagher and Sunny. There the grass will grow high around it and the nightshade twine over it as summer comes on. We won't think about it again until the first snowfall, months from now. Its removal is a timely symbol. Now we can walk on the flat grey-green stones that mark the entrance, the bands of grass between them yellow from their long imprisonment under the ramp, but almost visibly greening now to match the rest of the world.

The snow is really in rout, and today's strong warm wind will hurry it further into surrender. Where rearguard patches hang on, the fields have a leprous look. There are still white streaks under the ranks of trees on the heights. Dampness everywhere, in the air, underfoot. Small lakes of melted snow lie in the low areas of the fields, providing flocks of birds with bathing places. Our driveway has again become the Ganges River. Like the little boys in the Peterkin Papers, we must put on our india-rubber boots before venturing out. William had difficulty today taking soil samples from a 10-acre area, to be sent to the county agriculture office for testing so they can figure how much lime we need this year on the mowings; the ground was either still frozen or so wet and viscous that it clung to the spade and could not be mixed as directed. He dried out a potful in the oven, with Molly's little Roger and Stuart watching in enchantment at the actual baking of a mud pie.

A vast bank of fog in the valley this morning, and a thrilling roar from the swollen river, catapulting over the rocks. White water! There will be intrepid canoeists paddling furiously down its length today, and villagers hanging over bridges to cheer them on. It is a perilous sport. Every so often there is a drowning. If a canoe or raft overturns in these turbulent waters, the struggle to get free must be almost instantly successful, for the icy waters are literally paralyzing.

A raucous caucus of crows rouses us around six each morning. How delightful to wake to light once more instead of winter blackness! There are new birds showing up daily — a downy woodpecker nailing the maple trunk today. Their voices and cries and songs fill what was a silent void for too long. As the snow disappears, vast stores of new food are opened up, worms, insects, buds. Some species have deserted the feeding station entirely. The doves return, pecking at seeds strewn on the ground with total absorption, never swirling off skittishly with the jays and blackbirds at some real or fancied alarm.

The doves do rise and glide to the appletree when Eliza-cat approaches. Eliza flattens herself against the stones that border the bed of ferns, and sits motionless, the soft grey of her fur blending with the rocks, except for her prim white bib and boots. She has a most delicate head and sweetly innocent expression. She is light-boned almost as a bird herself. She is so timid that she spends most of her time avoiding Mr. MacGregor, the other cats, and alien humans, and her mew is soft and piteous. We think her sight is dimming, and sometimes she seems quite deaf. But her speed and agility when she springs at an unwary bird are simply incredible. When she brings me moles from the garden, I praise her prowess, but I cannot bear to see a mangled mass of feathers in her jaws. Birds are simply more precious on my scale of being.

So I go out now and pick her up from her ambush, bring her in and offer her milk and a helping of innocuous kitty-dinner. We both know this is a bribe and a temporary diversion from her natural predatory pursuits. She is seventeen years old, but her hunting days are not over yet.

White wind-flowers bloom in the sodden perennial borders and the pink nipples of peonies thrust themselves upward, all very spring-like. But the acres below the house are a fen crisscrossed with streams of water, and there are still grungy little snowpiles at the front door and all along the north lawn. We are not at our best. In fact, we are untidy and rather unclean, outside and in, and it is a time we pray no judgmental strangers come to call. Let them come a fortnight hence: by then, we expect to be presentable, perhaps even beautiful.

Even the celery and eggplant have ventured into light in my basement nursery. Only the stubborn green peppers remain underground. I spoke to them encouragingly this morning, sketching the delights of air and light and companionship they will enjoy aboveground. We shall see. I must not be too anxious.

A balmy day, a lovely day, everything responding perceptibly to the warm hand of the sun. I spent an hour picking up sticks from the south lawn — not just twigs and branches sundered from the maples by our boisterous winds, but also well-gnawed chunks of stove-wood snitched from the cache on the porch by Mr. MacGregor, some remnants of the Christmas tree, fragments of a smashed birdfeeder, debris from the firewood William chopped by the back door last November, the thousands of hulls of sunflower seeds — all the miscellaneous litter mercifully concealed by the snow all these months. The lawn looked more respectable with this cleared away, ready now to blush green overnight. I sat for a few moments savoring the improvement, happy to think of all the new life soon to flourish, the hills clad again in verdure, the meadows starred with flowers, the perennial borders glowing with color, the vegetable garden producing row on row — all that, and those horrible no-see-um black flies and strained muscles and weeds, weeds, weeds in my future too, if I care to be realistic about it.

William took out the caterpillar tractor, making giant sweeps across the vegetable garden, piling up remnants of snow in grimy banks at the southern end, with a view to hastening the melt, drying out the soggy soil, and, one day, ploughing and planting.

The single dove at the feeder, bobbing his head like a mechanical toy, ignores the bluejays and blackbirds, feeding close to the ground. Where can his mate be — nesting already? I trust it's that and not some injury or indisposition.

When I look down at the pond, I suddenly realize that the ice on the north side has melted, revealing a curve of open water for the first time this year. Now that's what I call an encouraging sign!

It happened between eight and nine o'clock this morning, the 20th of April. At eight the massive boulder still rested on the ice of the pond, but a large cracked area around it could be seen to have sagged perceptibly. When next we looked, the whole stout rock had vanished into the water. It would have been something to see and hear that splash, but we missed it, puttering around over a leisurely breakfast. When I realized what had happened, I sent up a resounding hurrah and danced about the kitchen table. It's not the trillion dollars I won from William, though that will come in handy. It is the dramatic symbol this represents of the final breaking of winter's grip. Now, even though we may have days when the snow flurries, the wind bites, and rutted roads freeze up again — and we will — the turning point has been reached. Soon we shall hear the peepers and the sun will grow stronger and the months ahead will teem with growth and life.

One of the gardening chores I find most satisfying is cleaning up the flower borders each spring. It is a task which must be done on time, and with care, for it is easy to clear away so enthusiastically that damage is done to tender perennials just emerging. It is best done by hand, rather than by hard-edged unfeeling tools. First the top layer of leaves comes off, dark, damp, decaying — entirely altered from last year's autumnal splendor, their death having harbored life all through the winter.

The daffodils, all in bud now, have poked up through this leaf cover, some of them carrying encircling leaves upward, the shabby brown remnant giving an incongruous air to the fresh green leaves, as if a smartly gowned young thing had walked out wearing an attic hat. When I remove the dead constricting leaves, the daffodils spring to freedom with apparent pleasure.

Down beneath a further layer of leaves and a scattering of twigs fallen from the maples are the iris in various stages of eruption. The tough bleached strings that are all that is left of last year's foliage catch at one's fingers and resist parting from the misshappen corms that lie half out of the earth like sleepers too lazy to cover themselves properly. The new green leaves are fragile if they have not been exposed to air, as easily torn as a lettuce leaf, and when once or twice I shear off a cluster of tips my distress is quite genuine and I apologize to the ravaged plant.

Peonies are even more delicate at this stage, and I tidy up around their clumps of rosy buttons with the same care given to great-grandmother's Limoges. The leftover stalks must be removed with precision, and the manure scattered up and heaped around the peonies where it will do the most good. "Heavy feeders," the garden books say of them, and that they are. Such a human phrase for a plant! At a time when people must be mindful of overtaxed resources, we can no longer be "heavy feeders" at one another's expense. But peonies know nothing of this, and will continue greedily consuming all they can get.

In the shadowed spaces bordering the house, daylily leaves lift their Gothic shapes in an early chartreuse color. They are the least trouble of all, proliferating casually and performing on schedule every July with a mass trumpeting of brassy color.

The faded Easter lilies and hyacinths from the florist are unceremoniously depotted and thrust in the ground in bare spots. Either they take hold or they don't — if yes, that's a sheer bonus. Lilies-of-the-valley, given me our first spring by Evelina Kent, are showing at the base of the stone steps by the southeast door. Their leaf color is a true ruby, no hint of the green-and-white pattern to come. Everywhere I encounter forsythia runners taking over aggressively, and hundreds of hopeful maple seedlings, all of which must be ruthlessly deracinated, along with the inevitable dandelions and "pussley" just getting a foothold. And grass, grass, grass where it isn't meant to be, though only to be expected when one lives in the midst of hayfields.

Three hours of work in the morning, two in the afternoon, and the improvement in the appearance of the borders is gratifyingly evident. And to boot there are five wheelbarrow loads of leaves, weeds and assorted debris to be dumped right onto the vegetable garden, to be turned under and begin a new cycle of nourishment and growth.

How the sun sparkled on the pond waters today! And with the coming of night we heard for the first time this season the frogs' chorus, a sound very like the quacking of ducks, hardly melodious, but how pleasing. In the background can be discerned the thin high fluting of the first peepers. Halleluiah, *hyla crucifer!*

Ho, what an end-of-April day! Warm as June, and it is a Saturday, so we take off with nothing on our consciences to join our friends Shep and Richard for a day of canoeing.

It is wonderfully apparent how, as soon as the weather turns clement, Vermonters with an almost audible sigh of bliss begin to shed their clothes. All the way over to Middlebury, we see entire families loafing or working in gardens, stripped virtually to the buff. On porch roofs, there are inert bodies stretched out to absorb maximum sun. "Can't blame them," I say, "after being swaddled all winter, but oh, dear, they're all risking skin cancer."

"That's not all they're risking," remarks William. "The ones on the roof will get shingles too."

In Middlebury we meet our friends, and in two cars, a canoe lashed atop each, we proceed to the Dead Creek Wildfowl Reservation.

We launch our canoes into the still brown water that runs an intricate system of channels for miles through tall clumps of reeds and bullrushes. Such a natural form of transportation, gliding almost soundlessly through the water! It is very warm, warmer than it has been since last summer, and quiet, except for cries of multitudes of birds — geese, ducks, gulls, red-winged blackbirds, rising in flocks as we paddle along. When we speak to one another we keep our voices low.

We come to a point of land, almost an island, where well-spaced pines have grown tall. There are four or five deer browsing in the shade. They lift their heads and watch us, wary-eyed, but we come almost to the shore before they vanish in a balletic wave into the farther woods. It is an idyllic picnic spot: musical breeze playing about in the tops of the pines, soft carpet of pine needles underfoot, moss and ferns to provide a dining area, absolute privacy. And this is no peanut-butter repast. In honor of the arrival of spring we have fresh Nova Scotia salmon, French bread and salad, cake and white wine. We eat it all with the greatest possible relish, enjoying the food, the place, the weather, the company, in a rare perfection of combination.

Conversation, at first lively and stimulating, tapers off to occasional companionable remarks. We lie back in the peace, the only activity the frantic struggle of a regiment of ants to transport huge burdens of cake crumbs up and down weed stalks and blades of grass. Later, we rouse ourselves to explore the woodland, finding tiny wild violets just peeking through the leaf mold, skunk cabbage, and other spring greenings.

The heat holds all afternoon. We find ourselves, in the sudden letting down of winter defenses, too indolent to take off and resume our paddling.

It is after five when we set out again in our canoes. Now the birds are dipping and swooping in their final flights before dusk. Thousands of wings move in complex traceries against the limpid air. Geese gabble, ducks quack, and from every tawny plume and tuft of their swampy thickets red-winged blackbirds, in their academic hoods, proclaim their presence with the preemptory call that invokes our northern spring.

The glistening drops from the tips of our paddles make silver rings in the slow dark water. Along a far bank we spy the sleek head of a muskrat swimming homeward.

We disembark, pull the canoes from the water, say farewell in the lingering warmth. It is still light on the road, and all the way back we marvel at the visible climb of green up the mountainsides, maples, birches, elms and beech leafing out jauntily. All this bright day, so insouciant for us, Spring has been hard at work.

Today I lifted out the tomato seedlings from their flats and placed them in a pragmatic variety of individual containers — large peat pots, coffee cans, cut-off bleach bottles and milk cartons. They all look somewhat stunned as a result of the operation, their young leaves drooping and their stems (what I've left aboveground) canting as if upright independence were beyond them. But in a day or two they should have recovered and be on their way to healthy and unobstructed individual growth. There are fifty of them — indubitably more than we need, barring a decimating blight, but when I look at their juvenile greenery I envision them in September, laden with scarlet globes, and I think large thoughts of *tomato salad, tomato juice, stuffed tomato, tomato-and-vegetable casserole, tomato chutney, tomato mince meat, tomato soup, tomato sauce.*

To Wells today by way of backroads, not a cloud in the sky, the sunshine truly warm, the countryside filled with signals of awakening. Southwest of Brandon, the meanders of Otter Creek are still flooded. Cornfields are transformed into gleaming expanses of water reflecting the azure sky. Gulls, white as crows are black, wheel above their temporary seas. What do they snatch up in their dives? Not clams, and jolly few fish amongst the drowned stubble, but frogs, of course, maybe a salamander or two. Along the road, ranks of willows are up to their knobby knees in water, branches every-witch-way. The road becomes a causeway with Dutch polders on either side — but those mountain shapes on every horizon prove it a never-Netherlands landscape.

Then on slightly higher ground, drier, where the woods come close, on the roadside bank is such a marvel that I stop the car and get out to look. It is a mille-fleurs carpet of trout lilies and bloodroot. The turk's-caps of the lilies are a pure sunny yellow, their sharply pinnate leaves dappled with a rich brown, and the white petals of the bloodroot stand out amongst them boldly. It is such a perfect and natural combination of shapes and colors, in such a prodigal display, that one can only be filled with gratitude as at an unexpected and tender gift.

The flowers stretch for several hundred feet along the road and extend far into the shadowed woods. If I had a trowel and bucket, would I dig some up? They would never be missed from such a host. But this is not my land; if it were, I'd be outraged if anyone made off with even a handful of these wildflowers, not because they were "mine," but because it would be a violation of perfection. Besides, if anyone passing by saw me, it would be a bad example, might invite others to do the same, ending in the ravagement of a whole fragile biota. There'd been hardly another car on the road all the way, but I knew that the moment I stooped to crime there would be a regular cavalcade of automobiles slowing down curiously. It would be exactly the same thing that happens in the Sahara, where, if one stops in a patently empty desert to answer a call of nature, instantly an entire tribe of Bedouins springs up, all eyes. No, conscience and public opinion would dissuade me, even were I supplied with tools, no matter how much I longed for a modest sample of this gold-and-white treasure to transfer to my own garden.

So it is back into the car and on the road again. Around the curve there is a porcupine carcass, a bristling hulk left by a swift vehicle, the quills still defiantly erect, the body not yet deflated by death. This is a creature not much subject to attack in the wilds, but Detroit is not daunted by hedgehogs.

This stretch is not prime agricultural land. Some fields are so boulder-strewn as to resemble pastures dotted with stone-white sheep. Some farms have gone to rack, some to ruin, some to both. Others struggle on with collapsing barns and rusty gaunt machinery. A few are kempt and running, and I give them a cheer as I pass. More cheers for the old houses where young couples earnestly tear off decomposed roofing, shore up sills, paint the front door blue. I love them for their archaic beards and long tresses, I love them for having survived the winter and for the plans they have made for the years to come.

Irish Setters says a sign, and immediately there is a trim house with outbuildings under the maples, and a family on the lawn — red-headed father, red-headed mother, red-headed child. Irish *settlers?* They look united and happy, and wave genially as I go by.

Unexpectedly I come upon a tall white frame relic from a time not so much distant as distinct from our own. Shutters missing, tower askew, it is a decaying inn set upon a knoll. Four Doric columns crowned with empty urns mark the driveway, cockeyed gazebos are strewn about what must have been a fine sweep of lawn, a fading sign proclaims *Green Mountain Mineral Waters, 25¢ a gallon.* It is the remains of one of those turn-of-the-century spas where one took one's liver to recover from endless 10-course dinners. The mineral waters are still there, but today nobody comes.

Lake Bomoseen and Lake St. Catherine are serene and glowing, unpeopled at this season, the clusters of tacky cottages still winter-closed. The waters are beautiful as any Alpine lake, with their inlets and islands and encircling hills. But one hill is utterly defaced, from crest to water's edge. It has been mined for slate, and the ugly black scarring is an insult to this scene. It dominates a whole section of the lake on the far side, and will never be mercifully overgrown with green. These evidences of slate-mining punctuate the landscape for a long painful stretch here. Hideous slag heaps, topped by cranes, rise up to disfigure the pastoral views in every direction. There are a number of quite handsome farmhouses here, notably two of weathered brick, but their outlook to the mountains is quite spoiled by the gross intrusions upon the flanks of the foreground hills. It must be because there is relatively little visual pollution in Vermont that one minds this so much. The slate floors in our house give us constant pleasure, but how dismaying to think their existence is owed to just such a mutilation of the gentle hillsides.

At the luncheon meeting, I sit next to a horsewoman who raises Morgans on Chittenden Mountain. She tells me about the spring foals, her eyes lighting up in a disciplined, weathered face. And I hear from the friend across the table that wild turkeys are once more to be seen in the woods in this county.

Back home — the trout lilies and bloodroot all closed up in afternoon shadow — to find William has harrowed the vegetable garden to a state of sumptuous chocolate-brown tilth, and that the vanguard of the barn swallows had flown in, earlier this year than any of our recorded dates.

The first weekend in May, thirty Quakers came for a "retreat," young couples, students, several infants, a few older Friends, bringing their pots of soup and home-baked bread and their sleeping bags. When they had all arrived and the practicalities had been companionably arranged, we entered into three hours of silence during which each could do whatever would nourish the spirit.

Some sat contemplatively leaning against tree trunks, lifting eyes to the hills. Others read — Fenelon or George Fox or Lao-tse. Others wandered meditatively. When we encountered one another, we communicated by smiles and occasional gestures. One who climbed the hill and looked down saw us scattered about, with Mr. MacGregor forming a connection as he trotted from one to another, communicating in his own friendly fashion with tail waggings.

All afternoon the birds were numerous and melodious, orchestrated by ranic sounds from the pond. The late sunrays touched the hills with that ineffable coral-rose color, and the Constable sky was traversed by successions of nobly formed clouds all luminous in pearly blues and silvers. An almost tangible peace pervaded hill and valley and encompassed us one and all. When we broke silence, a young girl who had sat most of the afternoon on a stone wall looking to the south, said to me, "I can't believe you *live* here," with a kind of awe in her voice. I assured her that there is never a day or an hour when I take it for granted.

After a merry communal meal, we sat in a circle speaking of our experiences during the silence. Elizabeth had followed the cloven hoofprints along the deer track into the spruce grove. William heard a mocking bird "lyrical as a nightingale" up in the sugarbush. Helen watched the leisurely progress of a fox along the ridge. Kitty and Jim ventured into the water at pond's edge, examining the floating masses of frogs' eggs. It seemed to have been a happy and moving time for everyone, with a heightening of awareness both physical and spiritual. In such a setting, nature is eloquent, and the light that pervades sky, hills and valley somehow enters the soul.

Our first spring here, having heard of the tradition that planting a pair of sarvis trees at the front entrance brings good fortune to the house, we put in two slender saplings. They are still slender, but now they are thirty feet tall and bring us special pleasure each spring — pillars of cloud, and, each fall — pillars of fire. Now in May they blossom not only at our door but throughout the woods and along every roadside. There is something magically fresh and innocent about that white amidst the gamut of spring greens. It is the white of new beginnings — christenings, first communions, commencements, bridals.

And yet the shadbush is a very ancient tree. It is a native of North America; fossil leaves have been found indicating that it grew here 50 million years ago. It is a member of the rose family, with two proper names: *Amerlancier aborea* and *Amerlancier laevis.* It also has quite a choice of common names: Service, or, in the Shakespearean pronunciation, Sarvis Tree; Serviceberry; Juneberry; Downy Shadblow; Shadbush; May Cherry; Sugar Pear; and Sugar Plum Tree.

Its wood is the heaviest that grows in the United States outside tropical areas, and it is a remarkably hardy tree, withstanding ice, snow and winds that fell surrounding lesser trees.

The shadbush greeted the Pilgrims with its sprightly blossoms their first spring in a strange land, and in 1623 they began to cultivate it for its fruits, which they made into tarts, jellies and puddings. George Washington, having a great fondness for sarvis trees, planted several near the main entrance columns at Mount Vernon; replacements for those original trees still grow in the same location. In Williamsburg, they were planted in formal gardens and along streets. The Duke of Argyll imported some to plant on his estate in England; several of these were later moved and now flourish in Kew Gardens in London. The British Royal Horticultural Society has bestowed its Award of Garden Merit upon this American cousin.

Though the fruits are often referred to as berries, they are actually little apples, as you can see if you take the trouble to dissect one. Archaeologists have found evidence that they were enjoyed by prehistoric man in North America, who couldn't have known that they have the highest vitamin C content of any tree fruit. As for flavor, Emerson is said to have declared Sarvis Pudding far superior to plum pudding. I've never had the patience to make Sarvis Pudding — the fruits are about the quarter of the size of cherries, with disproportionately large seeds. But when they are ripe — turning a glossy garnet color — I pluck a few each time I pass, savoring their delicious tartness.

Now at the height of their blooming, I break off a few small branches to bring inside, to study the arrangement of petals and stamens, and simply to enjoy when we cannot be outdoors. Each of the trees on this place has its own uses and charms, each is interesting in an individual way. The sarvis tree in springtime, at least for a few days of its flowering, it is easy to think — if not the queen — surely the princess of them all.

The Bird Lady came today. A Bostonian, she makes an annual visit to the village, not to its human inhabitants, but to the avian population. With her frizzled white hair, her offset eyes and Roman nose, her heavy tweed skirt and shapeless woolen sweater, she looks like a sheep in sheep's clothing.

Mr. MacGregor was invited to accompany her in her afternoon's exploration of our hill. About teatime they appeared at the kitchen door, both weary, she with her hair wind-ruffled above a square bronzed face.

We talked over the teacups of what she had seen — nothing special, towhees and killdeer and bobolinks. She had been shocked to find the new roads and houses in the second-home development uphill. "They've ruined it," she declared. "Barton Hill will never be the same."

Yesterday on the north side of the village she had seen bluebirds, but none here in spite of all the old fenceposts providing nesting places. I told her of the October day long ago when I had come home to another Vermont farmhouse to find the roof literally covered with bluebirds resting on the way south — a poetic and unforgettable sight. "Wouldn't see that now," the Bird Lady observed. "They're coming back after DDT, but not so numerous. I doubt they'll ever be."

Restored by tea and a half-hour's rest, she took her departure. "Your collie is well-mannered," she told me. "When I couldn't keep up with him, he stopped and sat down and waited for me to catch up. You know —" a fleeting grin reshaped her Yankee features momentarily and her keen blue eyes twinkled, "your hill has gotten a lot steeper in thirty years."

In the last few days we have marked off our rows and planted five kinds of lettuce, four kinds of carrots, as well as spinach and chard, radishes and turnips. We've sowed four kinds of peas along their wire fences. I've straightened up the asparagus rows, putting in 25 new roots, and planted three elderberry bushes. I've worked up a new border at the east end of the lawn, building up the bank, heaving stones into place for a low wall; with a whole untidy weed-patch eliminated, there is a delightful new neat effect, a proper setting for a dozen new Fairy Rose bushes, bleeding hearts and pansies, and clumps of wild sedum tucked in at the edges of the rocks. We have cut up and dug in scores of potatoes, and I, to the tune of William's protests that I am making too much work, put in 50 strawberry plants. He quotes Emerson: *A garden is like one of those pernicious machineries which catch a man's coat-skirt or his hands and draw in his arm, his leg, and his whole body to irresistible destruction.* A kind of mad urgency seizes us at this time each year — so much to be done and so little time to do it.

Yet when I kneel on the ground, crawling beside the furrows, dropping in the seeds and covering them to the prescribed depth, I do feel sacramental. I see within each seed a great trinity of faith, hope and love. Faith that it will indeed know when to begin its push to growth and what specific form it will take out of all the evolutionary possibilities. Hope that it will be blessed by friendly soil and the right portions of sun and rain. Love, because there must have been love in the design of creation, else there is no point in the ongoing cycle of birth and death and, every spring again, rebirth.

In the annual rush of garden chores I have once or twice allowed that transitory interval of the "spring ephemerals" to go by before I made time to go into the woods and discover these short-lived treasures, their season being the very brief one between the last snow-patches and the first plague of hot-weather insects. Today I left the vegetable rows behind and climbed over the stone wall to the soggy pasture where new grass is a luxuriant carpet of green.

Marsh marigolds bloom in all the boggy places in brilliant yellow splashes. On the day in May that Carl Linneaus celebrated his 28th birthday, long before he achieved fame as the innovative botanical classifier, he eagerly set out on foot for Lapland on his first journey of exploration of the natural world. He saw by the wayside few plants in flower, but one of them was the marsh marigold, called also cowslip. It was, he noted in his journal, sometimes called "Swedish caper" because people ate it instead of true capers. He added, "The report of its giving color to butter is certainly false." Color to butter? As a result of a tincture of marsh marigold petals added to it, or because the cows ate the blossoms? Linneaus does not say. A butter with that superb golden tone would be almost too luscious to eat. But I am tempted to pluck some of those tightly furled green buds that encircle the silk-petaled flowers, pickle them, and see how they do as capers.

Nearby, coltsfoot raises its leafless stalks crowned by heads like miniature sunflowers, with no sign yet of the indented leaves that appear after the flowers have finished blooming to give them their name. On the margin between stream and wood stand the sturdy willow bushes, their catkins now covered with a golden haze of anthers, that, caught in a certain slant of light, seems to light up the branches as for a festival. But it is no use trying to break off a branch — it takes a stout knife to cut through that toughness that makes the willow the ideal material for a woven basket.

Now entering the woods I spy the partridge berries, tiny, ruby globes aglow in their beds of shiny green leaves. The ground pine under foot has taken on a new shade of spring green, and there seems an infinite variety of plushy mosses. Beneath the spruce branches and in open spaces the ferns stand hand-high, their heads still curled in that tight pale spiral which contains all the makings of a plant that will at its height call to mind jungle size and color; right now they suggest nothing so much as a congregation of humble-shouldered Uriah Heeps.

At last I find the violets, infinitesimal delicate blue blossoms hiding in their leafy clumps. They are so small, so vulnerable, they implore you not to touch. I will not take naturalist Euell Gibbons's recommendation of eating both blossoms and leaves because half a cupful contains as much vitamin C as four oranges. They certainly were plucked in the past by Highland lassies, who had faith in an old Gaelic recipe which advised them to "annoint thy face with goat's milk in which violets have been infused, and there is not a young prince on earth who will not be charmed with thy beauty."

All unexpectedly, there amid the lichen-mantled rocks, is a scattering of those unmistakable mottled leaves, single and double, which mark a colony of dog-tooth violets. Ten or twelve are in blossom, small but with a regal air. Of course they are not violets at all, but members of the lily family. I like John Burroughs's name for them — he called them fawn lilies. That somehow seems to indicate the elusive character of this special flower, its grace, and its habitat. Not far off, peeping from the leaf mold at the roots of a lofty beech, are the shy hepaticas with their furry stems and lilac, pink, blue and white petals. Near the ruins of an old sugar house I discover a stand of pure white trilliums, and just beyond a few diminutive goldthreads with their deckle-edged leaves, and Solomon's Seal with its bell-blossoms, and the yellow-eyed May Apple hiding beneath its parasol leaves.

It is good I came in time to do homage to these prince regents whose reign is so very fleeting. Soon now the monarchical hardwoods will come into full leaf and with their crowns make such shade that few flowers will be found in this woodland domain until next year's spring.

We put our rhubarb patch pretty close to where the old Barton privy stood, and it took hold nicely. Every day or so I cut some of the ruddy stalks, remove the big coarse leaves with their load of poisonous calcium oxalate, and steam up a rosy compote mixed with brown sugar or honey in sufficient quantities to balance its astringency. Rhubarb — "pie plant," as it is often called around here — seems such an archetypal New England plant, reappearing so faithfully however harsh the winter almost as soon as the snow has melted, serving generations of Yankees as a spring tonic, yet it has quite an exotic history.

Rhubarb was used as a medicine by the Chinese as long as five thousand years ago; by the 14th century, it appeared in Europe, some carried along a tortuous route by way of the Indus and the Persian Gulf to the Red Sea and thence to Egypt, others by way of Aleppo and Smyrna. In 1653, China first permitted the Russians to trade along their frontier, and by 1704 rhubarb had become a monopoly of the Russian government. All rhubarb had to be passed by a government inspector, and Russian rhubarb came to have a very good name and a very steep price. At one time, its cost in France was ten times that of cinnamon and four times that of saffron. Its odd name holds some of its history. Rhubarb derives from a combination of two words: Rha, the ancestral name of the River Volga, and Barbaron, the Greek word for barbarian, alien, wild.

It has been a long journey to the Green Mountains, where it was brought by the earliest settlers. One often sees giant stands of rhubarb, with tall stalks of white flowers, in the vicinity of old cellar holes and abandoned gardens. Rhubarb should not be allowed to go to seed, however, if the next year's crop is to be at its best. An antique legend has it that if the plant goes to seed, there will be a death in the family before the year is out.

Our rhubarb hasn't a chance of going to seed, for what is not cut and eaten within the day will be brought in and prepared for the freezer, to serve as one of our favorite desserts all winter long.

In the early light, blue jays and grosbeaks spiral between maple tree and feeder. The sun illuminates their wings, their backs and breasts in swift flashings of color. The grass is now an intense new green, the maple leaves still suffused with their primal rose, the mountains to the west a purple backdrop against a clear blue sky. The birds are dramatically colorful, like actors in striking costume outshining the drab extras, the starlings, cowbirds and sparrows who remain at a distance while the stars take center stage. The jays are brilliant in their vibrant blue and black with patches of white in precise contrast, but the grosbeaks are opulent in sleek shadings of gold, brass, and ebony, their beaks a pure ivory, their eyes sparkling jet. There is a military air about the blue jays, not of recruits but of officers. The grosbeaks suggest Venetian merchants, their Renaissance garb advertising wealth and power, but a certain coarseness in the shape of head, in curve of beak, revealing a mercantile soul. The interweaving flight of these two dynasties — commandantes and mercantes — is like a vivid scene staged in an open theatre. One feels that if the squawks and shrilling were translated, the dialogue would be Shakespearean.

Temperatures in the eighties today. Mr. MacGregor in his heavy fur coat is panting, bedded down in the shade on the north side of the house. What heaven to work in this warmth without flies or mosquitoes. They will come, no doubt before the week is out, but these days are cherished for their special pest-free perfection.

The apple trees, contorted by nigh three score and ten winters, their limbs sprouting thickets of unpruned suckers, seemed the deadest things on the scene all these months of snow. Now there is a tentative rose-green flush along the twigs. There are actually incipient leaves and blossoms there, and a hope that this year, after last year's biennial rest period, there will be a decent crop.

This morning at nine o'clock, standing at the doorway, I saw a ruby-throated humming bird dart into the trumpet of a daffodil a few inches from my feet. The flower quivered under the swift intensity of the attack, then the humming bird was off on invisible wings to plunge his beak twice more into the golden cups down the row. As he sped around the ell of the house, a king bird watched from a telephone wire, wisely choosing not to compete with that electric irridescence in the thousand-yard dash. Humming birds with their 940 infinitesimal feathers have a wing beat of 200 per second when flying at 60 miles an hour, and they have the highest energy output per unit of weight of any living warm-blooded creature.

The red-winged blackbird population has never been so numerous, in the orchard, in all the maples, in and out of the tall lilac bushes. How brilliant are the shoulder bands of the male in his courting coat! One of the myriad spring miracles, the encarnadining of that segment of feathers just in time to make him irresistible to his modestly gowned mate.

When I went out to check on the new strawberry plants, I found nearly half of them strewn about the ground. I suspect those handsome blackbirds of this vandalism. No, that's too strong a word — doubtless they spied those new green leaves in the fresh brown earth of the garden and tweaked them out for a possible buried seed at the tail of each. It had rained a bit during the day, so the roots did not seem entirely dried out. I replanted them prayerfully (all but a few which had vanished), reflecting that perhaps William is right in thinking a strawberry bed is just too much.

Dinner is later each evening now. We work outside until nearly seven, then retire to the terrace, drinks in hand, to watch the marvelous late light illuminating the valley and coloring the hills. It really is a spell-binding scene, and always a little different.

At this stage, the leaves on most of the trees are still young (those on the maples the size of a baby's hand), and this makes for the most achingly lovely and subtle effects, a kind of dream quality in the variety of greens from citron to jade which will later be lost in a great sweeping mass of ripe greens without these elegant distinctions. In the evening light, these shadings are even more striking, and the pond takes on a sheen that it saves for just this hour.

The birds are busily flitting about and we try to identify their calls. The bird books are of no help whatsoever. There is one call that is truly a liquid note — exactly like a quiet fountain splash — that is part of the cowbird's repertoire. The swallow population is increasing but will not be at its highest until more insects are available. The blue jays, our greedy boarders all winter, have mostly deserted us now for the privacy of the deep woods where they will raise their families.

Daffodils are everywhere. One bed of them, the first I ever put in here, survives poor drainage and invading quack grass to blossom so robustly that they seem to glow with a collective inner light so radiant it almost hurts to look upon them. I love their ancient names

— asphodel and Lent lily — and the thought that medieval ladies made yellow dye from the blossoms with which to dye their hair and eyebrows.

If I could choose my birthday, it would be this time, mid-May. But oh, to think that in just seven weeks the sun will reverse its power and the days will begin to grow shorter. No, I shall not think.

A day of firsts. First lawn mowing. First scarlet tanager. First plants up from the basement and out to be hardened off. First ice cream cone. First iced tea. First mosquitoes. First swim in the pond.

Day follows day of unbelievable warmth. The upper soil dries and cracks, crumbling in the hand. But the trees and grass, drawing on the deep store of moisture below, burgeon and blossom. The Alcotts, the dairy farmers with whom we share a boundary, predict a dry summer and glance uneasily at the new houses on the hillside above. "Those second-home people don't know about living in the woods. Just one of them, careless with fire —"

White lights up the green everywhere. Shadblow petals have drifted to the forest floor, but other bloom arrives in succession. Locust trees are so hung about with pearly clusters that a grove of them sheds a baroque luster upon the whole vicinity. False Solomon's Seal populates wide stretches of hillside, thrusting vibrant white struts upward in ranks along the road. Cherry-tree blossoms seem no kin of their civilized cousins, their white sprays arching boldly from slender branches. Patches of Bladder Campion and Fool's Parsley take temporary possession of the meadows. Lower down, wild strawberry petals and flowering briars promise a summer harvest. In the villages, of the venerable lilac bushes some of the tallest are the white ones, reaching up twenty feet or more and spreading outward in graceful sweeps. Snowball bushes and mock orange shrubs display their simple charms. Old spirea bushes are whitest of all, covered with thousands of doll-size lace doilies.

A welcome rain last night. This morning everything steaming in the renewed heat, and dandelions in such profusion they are an occupying army. There is so much gold everywhere — dandelions, cowslips, wild mustard — one would think Midas had touched the land. But the daffodils droop, and I put in pansies and forget-me-nots to fill the borders.

Our lilacs proffer wizened little clusters which all burst into fragrance later, but for some reason they are always much later than those in the valley — Woodstock, Bethel and Rutland are always properly lilaced for Memorial Day, but our late-bloomers are sometimes still blossoming on the Fourth of July.

Maple leaves are now full-size, and the countryside takes on a more uniform green. How quickly it happens, especially in a year like this with unwonted stretches of warmth to encourage and bless the emerging growth. We are grateful, but also wary. We know this benevolence may be replaced within hours by a killing frost, a catastrophic windstorm. There were temperatures below freezing every month of the year of 1816 in Vermont.

Last year we had such a parlous apple crop that I actually had to go to the Brandon orchard and pay to be allowed to pick enough for our supply of applesauce. Three years ago the spring was so nastily cold and wet the bees were not able to pollinate what blossoms the battered trees put forth. This year we rejoice, so far. Every apple tree still standing in our orchard, which annually suffers a toll of one or two ancients which split and crash to the ground, is alight with a profusion of flowers that would seem impossible, almost indecent, in such overage and neglected trees. From a haggle of arthritic beldames they are transformed into a joyous bridal party. Even the odd trees along the old pasture fences are flaunting their garlands. I counted thirty-one apple trees in full bloom today. And when I went and stood quietly in the tall grass under the white and pink boughs of the orchard, I heard, Oh, with what thanks, the low thrumming, humming, drumming of thousands of bees, going about their immemorial fertility rites.

The unseasonable warmth continues. Outdoor work is a visual joy, with sunlight bathing the land, the sky either a clear azure or a china blue, with calm processions of cumulus clouds. If life were but a picnic, there would be nothing but pleasure in such halcyon weather. But this misplaced midsummer makes us anxious. The soil has dried out rapidly and now is compacted on the surface and to a surprising depth below. Farmers who were happy to get their corn in earlier than usual now squint at the sky and repeat the old saw, "a rainy May means a barn full of hay." Dairy farmers depend on hay to a vital extent here where the pasturage season is relatively brief. Last year there was a shortage, with prices going up to more than a dollar a bale, and Canadian hay trucked down at great expense. For the first time, Justin Alcott, who takes a portion of our hay each year in return for mowing our acres, has scraped up nearly every straw from our barn floor, leaving only a bit for the horses and none for garden mulch. He did bring a load of spoiled hay, rich with dung, which will be enough for about half the garden; some has already been arranged in the new strawberry bed, which I'm glad to see is responding nicely.

Franklin Farnsworth made me fifteen bean poles of peeled and sharpened saplings from his woodlot, and they have been erected in a semicircle of tepee shapes, with five kinds of bean seed round them. Squash and zucchini have been bedded near them in little mounds. These large visible seeds are a pleasure to plant; each individual one is so full of potential, so easy to put in the ground at a ratio something like the expected results. Carrots and lettuce seeds are so wasteful, impossible to "sow thinly" as the packets instruct and requiring such tiresome thinning out of their crazy excess. A row of dill goes in companionably alongside, and some marigolds and borage. Next is the brassicae patch — cabbage, cauliflower, broccoli and brussels sprouts, out of the cold frame and into the ground now, looking rather lost in space at this stage but quite capable of taking over aggressively in a few weeks. We must water everything daily, unprecedented at this date when we are generally groaning about too much moisture.

There has been much splashing about in and upon the pond these days, the little boys launching canoe and dinghy and noisily navigating in circles. Bridget goes swimming two or three times a day, encouraging Mr. MacGregor, no swimming enthusiast, to dog-paddle. There is no sign of the trout we put in last fall. But bulrushes are creeping forward from the shoreline into the water. We think of our neighbor's pond, almost entirely choked by rushes, and ponder the advisability of enlisting the aid of a family of ducks — the foxes would no doubt approve that idea.

Last night we dined in South Strafford, the conversation largely dwelling on solar energy, wind power, and taxes. As we started home, the lunar eclipse was just beginning. We watched for an hour, driving along slowly, the earth's shadow cutting into the golden globe with a kind of chilling relentlessness. Of course we know what is happening, that it is a temporary phenomenon, but there remains in the dark corner of one's limbic corrugations a primitive awe, a tremulous question: *What if...?* that no amount of rational explanation can dispel. The planets are so plainly beyond our ordering, no matter how many human foot prints now lie forever on the surface of the moon.

The pace of the eclipse is measurable by the eye, a weird speeding up of the tempo to which we are accustomed in the phases of the moon. We stopped by a bend in the river and watched the shadowed sector of the moon grow orange, an unnaturally warm color for that cold dead sphere. Then we hastened home to get out the binoculars and look at the marvel from our terrace. All the warmth of the early evening had vanished. The air was now crisp and chill, and the stars extraordinarily brilliant and numerous. William knows them by name, and greets Arcturus and Orion with respectful familiarity here in the mountains as he has so often at sea. At the moment of total eclipse, the moon seemed enormous behind its dark veil, a glowing cinder, quite unlike its usual reflective self. Through the binoculars, it was awesome. We could not have had a finer view, the heavens so boundlessly open overhead, so utterly clear. We could scarcely believe the newspapers next morning, reporting that skies had been overcast throughout the northeast and the lunar eclipse invisible to millions of disappointed observers.

The Memorial Day weekend has been filled with activities — a village parade, speeches, a band concert, a chicken barbeque on the green. At home we kept up the rhythmic round of spring tasks. William and Skip transplanted poplar trees which had grown in two years from twelve-inch rooted cuttings to six-foot heavily leafed younglings with stubborn and extensive root systems. They will go to join the triple line of trees we have been planting north and west along road and driveway to form one day a windbreak and snowfence. The Bartons farmed this place so thriftily that they cleared everything off the fields and pastures surrounding the house, except for a few maples and the cottonwood and a line of elms. I feel a little guilty, planting trees where the land was cleared with such labor, but also I wonder why the Barton men never seem to have admitted that they lived directly in the path of the incessant west wind and their house could have used more protection. How terribly bleak those winters must have been! The women must have minded. One of the last Barton sons born in this house told me, "My grandmother said she lived here for forty years and the wind never stopped blowing once." Well, the willows and poplars and spruce and Russian olive we are putting in now may not make all that difference in our lifetime, but future inhabitants could be grateful.

The corn is planted, in rows which look regular but will prove not to be once the leaves come up. Tomato plants, long-leggedy beasties, are eased into compost-filled holes along a series of fencings, protected by milk cartons and ramparts of soil. Finally, zinnias and asters are sown in the cutting garden and the long chore of mulching with layers of the *New York Times* and old hay is begun.

There is a sense of relief and accomplishment that everything is at last *in*. We could enjoy this brief period of grace if only we were not bedevilled by alternating visions of the outcome.

One set of dreams conjures up exemplary green rows of unblemished peas and beans, sturdy regiments of sweet corn, fountains of scarlet tomatoes the size of basketballs, not to mention hills of rotund squash and pumpkin, teeming ranks of broccoli and their cousins, spinach and carrots rivaling the pictures in the seed catalogues.

Almost immediately, however, in the mind's eye the scene shifts to a nightmare view: the garden in successive stages of desolation, brought on by frost, hail, forty days of rain, forty days of drought, armies of slugs, phalanxes of cutworms, hosts of Japanese beetles, every variety of mold and fungus, ravenous deer, victorious woodchucks and racoons, trampling livestock, imported blights hitherto known only in Mozambique and the Upper Nile.

It is enough to drive one to the borders of schizophrenia, but fortunately Mother Nature impartially goes about her business of arranging something between total success and total disaster. There will be some triumphs and some failures, perhaps minimal peas this year but a bounty of cucumbers, only a handful of acorn squash but a superabundance of potatoes. It balances out just often enough to keep the gardener going year after year, expecting surprises and thankful for whatever makes it from seed packet to dinner table.

Summer

Yesterday's blessed rain expanded into a prolonged downpour, pounding, flattening the earth's new growth, refilling the diminished streams, washing out dirt roads, drowning the garden. It waned at intervals, then fell upon us with renewed intensity, sometimes accompanied by lightning of a crackling, blazing intensity fit to announce the arrival of Beelzebub and all his hosts.

It was nearly eleven o'clock and three of us were returning, tired and damp, from a day-long meeting in Plymouth. The Bronco clattered and groaned up the hill. Visibility was reduced to a few feet, water streamed across the windshield, vast puddles were black mirrors in the road. Almost home, we took the road that parallels Barton Hill and loops across to join it. One stretch is virtually a causeway, climbing steeply with high banks sloping sharply down at each side. Just here, where the guardrail begins, the accident happened. Across the railing, into the blurred dazzle of our headlights, a deer leapt in one beautiful fatal bound, directly into the path of the car. I saw it in a sickened instant before it came into bright focus, but my cry could not alter the sequence. There was no time at all to stop. The impact had that density of sound which communicates instantly the gravity of the shock.

William braked, turned the key, and jumped out, Bridget just behind him, to look in the black streaming night at what injury had been done. It was a very young deer, looking piteously small in the headlights. I did not get out. Not that I minded getting wet, but I am not very good about watching dying.

There was no blood. William examined the preposterously slender legs and found them unbroken. The deer's head was turned upward, its eyes staring into the glaring eyes of the metallic monster that had struck without warning. Its rib cage, the fur roughened and dark, rose and fell in long, excruciating shudders. The eyes held a red glow which flared and ebbed and flared again as if consciousness of horror alternated with obliterating shock.

What could we do? Lifting the body into the car could be fatal. Leaving the deer to suffer in the teeming rain was too heartless. The only course seemed to be notification of the game warden. William stroked the matted shoulder and spoke a few words of helpless apology to the deer.

We were home and at the telephone within five minutes. The warden, roused from sleep but calm and efficient, promised he would be there shortly. He would take care of the carcass — yes, the deer was undoubtedly dead. "They usually live about ten minutes after being hit, even if you can't see any injury." We could do nothing more than trail off to bed, trying to put that spotlighted scene out of our minds.

In the morning, going back over the road in feckless sunshine, there was no sign of the deer. The warden will add its dried blood to his collection, to be given to gardeners as fertilizer or to be sprinkled on the young green lettuce and broccoli to discourage other living, hungry deer from nibbling, for, it seems, they prefer not to dine on the blood of their own.

We are green as Ireland, and as damp. In all the mowings hay shoots up visibly, and weeds come on like an army of Alexander the Great. Field cress is rampant in all the vegetable rows. We pick a bit, adding its sharp savor to the tiny new leaves of lettuce and spinach for salads, but cannot possibly utilize that entire saucy proliferation; it will have to be dug out. Among the familiar plagues of chickweed, purslane, dock, ragweed and mullein are the thick grey-green spoon-leaves of borage, self-sown throughout the vegetable rows from a nearby perennial border. These I try to salvage, using the tenderest leaves for salads and transferring the sturdier plants to a neat line at the edge of the vegetable rows, where later on they will furnish a prolonged bloom of small, fervently blue, star-shaped flowers which masses of bees will frequent like topers at the neighborhood pub.

I keep well in mind the lines from Shakespeare:

Now 'tis the spring, and weeds are shallow-rooted;
Suffer them now, and they'll outgrow the garden,
And choke the herbs for want of husbandry.

Of course it was Margaret, King Henry VI's queen, who was speaking here symbolically of the untrustworthy Duke of Gloucester, but the Bard knew whereof he spoke in respect to husbandry.

It's true that some of our infinite variety of weeds are still shallow-rooted and relatively easy to discourage. But not the grasses, which keep trying to reclaim the garden in its entirety. They are well-nigh indomitable. I read not long ago of a four-month-old rye plant grown in a greenhouse which had a combined length of roots that measured 387 miles. I believe this might be true of most grasses in Vermont. They are our top crop, they love it here, they intend to stay.

I have to remind myself of Senator John James Ingalls's work, *In Praise of Blue Grass,* in which he said, back in 1872, "Grass is the forgiveness of nature, her constant benediction...Should its harvest fail for a single year, famine would depopulate the world."

And what could be more beautiful, this emerald green stretching in every direction after the early June rain?

If it would just stay out of the garden...

It is hard not to be indignant when on the 6th of June at breakfast-time the thermometer registers 40 degrees. O, pity the brides who have chosen this date for an outdoor wedding! It is a miserable day, a vicious wind snarling out of the west, everything dank and chilled. Nothing for it but to fire up the wood range and bake a comforting batch of whole-grain bread.

The house is throbbing with Madge's and Lydia's children — seven here at the moment. When it rains, there are hay fights in the barn, anagrams or player-piano concerts in the living room. When it shines, there are tree climbing, excursions to the woods, water fights in the pond. The little boys are always wet or muddy, heads richly sprinkled with hayseed. Five of them, squealing and giggling, packed into the doghouse Mr. MacGregor occupies only on occasion. Their hilarious eruption from door and window was one of the memorable sights of this happy month.

In the east pasture where we picnicked tonight there were ten children mounting the back of the immense granite outcropping we call the Whale Rock. Their faces alight with camaraderie, the cousins' voices mingled in spontaneous chorus. Here in this mountain sea of green grasses, they brought to mind a fleeting comparison with those Mediterranean tales of boys sporting in the sea astride playful dolphins.

The sun, soon to be at its northernmost apogee, is setting in a molten effusion in what seems an unaccustomed sector of sky and hills. The twilight is prolonged; a crescent moon is suspended near Venus against a pale scrim of sky.

A shout as the children discover the first fireflies. They tumble off into the high grass, pursuing the dancing lights in joyous confusion. Darkness deepens, the glow of the fireflies intensifies. There has never been such a brilliant choreography spangling the whole hillside. The children cry out in wonder and delight, capturing a few in eager hands, peering into the crevices of their imprisoning fists to marvel at the pulsing glow within, then freeing them with upward gestures.

How reluctant they are to come to bed! It is a night for all of us to stay up, to stay out, to stay in its course.

Purples and blues everywhere now, with episcopal violet shades amongst the iris, outsize royal blue bachelor's buttons along the terrace, virgin's tears with their soft sky blue tinged with pink at the foot of the sundial, and a bank of baby blue speedwell near the barn. Our late lilacs unfurl at new heights, higher than our low roofline at east and west, in every hue from palest mauve to Tyrhennian purple. Out in the marshy reaches of the west pasture, stiff-stemmed and regally colored, the wild flags keep to themselves. Amethyst sprays of vetch appear in all the meadows, as they did long ago in Concord. Thoreau wrote of them: "From the lane in front of Hawthorne's, I see dense beds of tufted vetch, for some time taking the place of the grass in the low grounds, blue inclining in spots to lilacs like the lupines...It is affecting to see such an abundance of blueness in the grass. It affects the eyes, their celestial color. I see it afar, in masses on the hillsides near the meadow, much blue, laid on with so heavy a hand..."

We are 18 for dinner one night, 20 for lunch next day — four generations in amiable interaction. Four dogs and a few extra cats weave in and out of the human stream, keeping track of all the two-leggeds and four-leggeds.

The common field elm was known to the Greeks, mentioned by Pliny and Vergil. In the reign of Henri IV, at his express wish, hundreds of elms were planted along the highways of France by his minister Sully, and the elm came to be called "sully" or "Henri Quatre" in memory of these illustrious planters. Many of these trees survived into the time of the Revolution, and in Burgundy, there were elms with trunks four to five feet in diameter, "which, though hollow, yet supported heads capable of sheltering some thousands of men."

The American elm, as we know it in Vermont, never achieved such majestic proportions, but planted along village streets it bestowed its own democratic grandeur of columns and arches, filtered light and green shade. The loss of thousands of elms to implacable disease has left these villages and towns exposed and naked, looking older and starker, revealing where architectural errors and failures of upkeep had been charitably cloaked by the presence of those gracious trees.

On our main street, the elms have fallen, one by one, yet there still stood until recently a stately specimen next to what was once the Methodist church and is now the Youth Hostel. There came a day when one lane of the street was closed off as a crew of woodsmen went to work with their ropes and powerful tools, for the elm was dying, nearly dead, now posing a threat to the building and to the traffic that flowed beneath it.

All day the men worked, lopping off branches, and all day the people of the village came to watch, to remember and to mourn. The tree, set out when the church was built, had been planted by a man great-great-grandfather to many of them. When at last the dismemberment was finished, the massive trunk severed, the pieces of the corpse were trucked away and there was nothing left but a raw stump and mounds of sawdust. People counted the rings, and picked up bits of bark and twigs, studying them as if they might contain some revelation of the life of that tree which had paralleled so much of the life of the village. It was a death keenly felt.

Most fittingly, in this week's valley newspaper there was an obituary for the elm. At its death, it was 152 years old.

William has mowed a path to the pond, but on either side there are flowering marvels so distracting that the walk downhill and back up again after a swim is slowed to turtle's pace. In the pond itself, the top inch of the water is the temperature of a 10-minute-old cup of tea, but just below lie spring-fed depths that enfold the body in liquid ice. Nothing could be more restorative on one of these 85-degree days when it is simply too hot to pursue one's appointed tasks. It is bliss to float, surrounded by water, sky and hills, everything shades of blue and green.

Daniel catches a young frog and brings it to show me. When he opens his hand, I have just time to glimpse the pearly roundness of the frog's belly before it springs up and over into the water with a splash. We tread cautiously along the shore and spy a giant fellow, its coat exactly the copper-green of the reeds amongst which it crouches with starting eyes and pulsing throat. Daniel makes a grasp, but the wily creature, with an instantaneous and astonishing elongation of its body, streaks out of reach, diving deep into the dark waters where it cannot be discerned.

We see salamanders darting through the water like their own shadows, and everywhere floating gelatinous masses of frogs' eggs. There is an occasional croak from somewhere in the bulrushes, but the frog chorus is saving itself for the evening concert when, with the obligato of the peepers, their performance rings with notes of cello, pipe and bass viol multiplied by hundreds, far across the valley.

The heat continues, and the sun seems to stand still at midday. Aten, the sun god worshipped by the pharaoh Akhenaten and his Nefertiti, was portrayed as a disk with rays arrowing toward the earth; each ray ended in a tiny human hand, some of them holding the *ankh*, symbol of life. These days, one can almost see these rays inspiriting the garden, the little hands coaxing the plants ever higher. Peas are beginning to climb their fences, rosettes of potato leaves appear above the straw, lines of spinach thicken and grow tall, the largest tomato plant is in flower. These compensate for the melon plants which resented transplanting so deeply that they died, and for the overtender eggplants, so strikingly green when set out, now sulking with leaftips bleached by one or two near-frosty nights early on.

Justin Alcott is haying his mowings along the branch of the river, but promises he will get to ours soon. The moment of peak quality goes by so quickly, and already we see our green timothy and clover begin to be tinged with gold.

What seemed at first glance a new species of lichen on the warm tumbled stones of the pasture wall is revealed as a colony of young ladybugs. They are sunning in a glossy vermillion mass which constantly disintegrates at the edges and reforms with the busy venturing of individuals. Some are pinhead size, others more developed, but not yet winged.

Five years ago, a thousand ladybugs arrived in the post office box, done up in a muslin bag. They were placed according to instructions overnight in the refrigerator, to "calm" them, then released in the garden to do their advertised work of consuming destructive insects. By the next day they had all vanished. Apparently all we had done was provide a free meal for the swallows. Occasionally we would see one or two, not in the garden, and in winter there would be a small sluggish party of them inside my sunlit study window. But the great migration had evidently been eastward, and successful, for now there are countless ladybugs at home on the rocks and in the hiding places of a long grey line of stone wall. I doubt if reciting verses ("Ladybug, ladybug, fly away home") will have the slightest effect in getting them back to the garden where their ancestors were supposed to go to work as efficient, non-polluting pesticides.

A pair of Canadian strangers stopped by unannounced. We dropped our trowel and axe and led them to the terrace where they sat at the parasol table and gazed down the valley. It was a day of June perfection. The pond sparkled. Little Wilcox and Corporation Mountain rose plushly green against the sky, Rochester Mountain sunning itself like a contented cat to the east, and to the west Mount Horrid and Cape Lookoff Mountain angled dramatically to Brandon Gap.

The husband and wife gave hardly a glance at the panorama before them as they sipped iced tea and carried on a rather testy commentary on the subject of Vermont ancestors (theirs and mine, no relation) who chose to go to Canada at the time of the American Revolution, thereby becoming United Empire Loyalists.

Finally the visitors from Ottawa fell silent for a moment. The husband's eyes swiveled uneasily from east to west.

"Tell me," he said, "don't you feel *hemmed in* by all these hills?" Flatlanders!

Last night Duncan told us of the offer he has to work in California. It is tempting — a position in a new firm, offering considerable responsibility and a quite surprising salary. He is young, highly competent; he enjoys a challenge. Of course he is attracted to the proposal. But California is a continent away, with a philosophy and style of living which seems from this distance to be antithetical to the way we think and do here. Duncan is not over-articulate, but we know what he means when he says, "It would be leaving everything Vermont means."

It is an old quandary. There are no greener fields than Vermont's in midsummer, but there are rocks in those fields, and long deep winters here, and crazy weather and PhD.s pumping gas and, for many, poverty which, if it is not accepted, can only be defied by moving elsewhere. From the beginning, almost as soon as they cleared a field and set up a dwelling, Vermonters, quite a number of them, have looked west, taken up their tools, and moved on.

Matthew Lyon, who came from Ireland just before the Revolution, was beside Ethan Allen at the capture of Fort Ticonderoga, served with the Vermont militia at Bennington and Saratoga, and became secretary to his father-in-law, Vermont's first governor. Matthew bought up land confiscated from loyalists (including some of my own ancestors' property), set up grist and saw mills, an iron works, and a paper mill, edited a newspaper, and was elected to Congress. It would seem he had put all his energies and his heart into these Green Mountains. Yet in 1797, Lyon sold all his Vermont property and took off for western Kentucky, where he did nearly the same thing all over again. The migration which went on all through the next century drained Vermont of some of its best citizenry.

But always there remained a core of obstinate land-lovers who refused to leave, who seemed almost to glory in contending with hostile elements and overcoming enough of the obstacles to security and comfort to survive. It could not have been lack of courage or gumption that kept them from joining the westward movement, for courage and gumption they needed in full measure to remain. And those who stayed, along with those who chose to come and throw in their lot with them, have given this state its character, not without its flaws, surely, but of a stamina and independence not easily come by and not so easily found elsewhere.

A shine comes into Duncan's eye as he speaks of what he would be doing in California, a kind of hunter's gleam. We think we know what his decision will be.

The tenderest summer evening, taking on nursery hues of pink clouds in blue sky. Venus is dazzling, high in the west. The pond is utterly smooth, a true silver. From the spruces at the crest of the hill road a pair of owls wing silently, silhouetted against the sky. One mouseling I know to be beyond the terror of their attack.

Stefano brought it in to the kitchen before supper, a perfect wee grey creature not much longer than an inch, its tail absurdly small.

It lay in Stefano's somewhat grubby hand, curled in embryonic shape, eyes still unopened. There was the faintest twitch of life.

"He's not dead! Can't we put him in a box and feed him milk with an eye dropper?"

"Stefano, he's too young. We've nothing small enough to serve for nursing anyway. We couldn't possibly keep him alive. Just handling him would be too much for him."

It takes a long time to convince Stefano that rescue is not possible. It is dreadful to be so old and knowledgeable about such things, so darkened by memories of failed life-saving efforts in the past, and to have to pass on this negativism to the hopeful young.

"Then where shall I put him?"

"Lay him gently in the high grass. He'll go to sleep and not wake up."

Slowly Stefano walks out, cradling the doomed baby. I see him kneel to make a tiny space amongst the stalks of timothy. He does not rise immediately. At thirteen he is a cheerful agnostic, so he can't be praying, not consciously. He comes back to the supper table, and eats with his usual appetite. But he speaks very little all evening.

Now at nine o'clock, the pink and the blue have faded in the west. Now the owls are the only moving things between sky and meadow.

Early this morning, Justin and two of his sons came up the hill with tractor, mower and hay wagon. All day they have worked tirelessly under the baking sun, starting on the upper mowing.

The broad acres are so beautiful, uncut; you can follow the passage of every breeze as it undulates across the green expanse, changing the intensity of its luster. Now precise inroads are made in the perfection of its surface. The hay falls in windrows under the clattering machine. We are thankful the job is being done, thankful for this prolonged spell of perfect haying weather. Yet it means a drastic change in the appearance of the land, a cutting down of thousands of grasses that were so triumphantly living and growing.

Of course the grasses will grow up again, of course this hay will serve to nourish Alcotts' cows and our horses. Nevertheless, there are inevitable intimations of conquering armies mowing down ranks of the unarmed, and of Father Time scything all before him.

On the first day of July, weeding the ajuga and fairy roses, I heard a cricket. There was no mistaking his little bell-note, which is at once cheerful and melancholy. The almanac warns that it is six weeks to frost from the first cricket's voice. Good heavens, that would be mid-August! And we have barely thawed out from winter yet...No, this must be a precociously early sentinel, not to be taken literally. Yet two days later, I heard it again, in the hay mulch surrounding the cabbages, and the same pang flashed through my viscera. There is something that cannot be dismissed in that folk wisdom, though it so often proves fallible. The cricket, agile and wary with his black soutane and musical legs, jetting from haystalk to daisy under the midsummer sun, is a harbinger of frost, snow, sleet, ice, and the destruction of all this busy, fruiting, golden world through which he travels in high summer, sending forth his message of summer's end.

Now the hay has been tedded and well-dried, with miraculously no cloudburst to drown it, no moisture beyond the nightly heavy dews. The baling machine has gathered up the cuttings and spewed them out in corded bales. A hard-working band of Alcotts follows along to load the hay on the truck, get it to the barn and pile it bale on bale in loft and bays. Dora Alcott is right there with daughters and sons who have come back home for the haying season, and a grandchild or two old enough to ride along and learn how it's done. One grand-baby sleeps on our sofa, waking when his mother comes to feed him. William helps too, standing on the truck and tossing up bales to the boys who are stacking them in the barn where shafts of sunlight swirl with hay dust. I make lemonade by the gallon and take it out to the parched and sweating workers. It is a tremendous labor, which must be perfectly timed in all its elements, and it is carried on year after year with great good humour and no complaints.

Hundreds of cars, brimming with sunburnt children, converge upon the field where the anniversary of that subversive document, the

Declaration of Independence, is to be celebrated. The last sea green expanse of sky subsides into grey, and Venus glowing in the west is joined by tentative attendant stars. Almost at the moment night can be said to have taken possession of the heavens, a salvo of explosions rings out and streaks of fire hurl themselves vertically to expand into dazzling patterns, hanging for an instant in phosphorescent splendor, then arcing earthward as their glory burns out. Catherine wheels spin in dizzy blazings near the ground, vast golden chrysanthemums bloom for a matter of seconds high above us, kaleidescopic showers of red, yellow, blue, green and white burst magnificently against the blackness, trailing thousands of sparks while clusters of light swim downward in the shapes of twisting fish and frantic spermatazoa.

A great public Ah! goes up at each extravagance. The noise is dreadful. Every firework is sent off with maximum tumult, to explode again and again up in the air, accompanied by siren shrieks and piercing whines. Reverberations thunder from the enclosing hills. How agitated the deer must be, huddled in the high forest, at the sound of what must seem a titanic hunting party. One cannot escape the echoes of old wars and the most recent murderous firepower in Vietnam, Afghanistan, Beirut. This patriotic display in the Vermont hills with all its overwhelming blasts is too loud, too bright, too fierce, too close to suggesting the real thing, the terror of helpless civilians and trapped soldiers under countless attacks experienced in nearly every corner of the earth since we learnt about firepower.

"The Chinese really started something," says William.

"It would be beautiful if it didn't have any sound," observes Adrian.

After the ear-splitting crescendo of the grand finale, in the ringing quiet we climb back into the car. "What did you think of it?" we ask Margot, who has seen fireworks at Jones Beach and in Rome.

Her reply holds more than the wisdom of her fifteen years: "They're all the same," she says.

There's something about a starling that isn't very darling. There's a scruffy look about him, his black rusty suit pulled out of an old trunk, decidedly a hand-me-down. If his eyes weren't beady, you'd say they were shifty. He has none of the dash of the red-winged blackbird or the saving iridescence of the purple grackle. Most of his feathers have cowlicks. His voice is distinctly ill-bred and his manners not ingratiating. Even his Latin name — *sturnus vulgaris vulgaris* — betrays the lack of esteem in which he is held by ornithologists, who are apt to describe him as "gregarious, aggressive, often an abundant pest in parks, suburbs and farms; song largely squeaky notes, harsh or rasping, although capable of giving good imitations of other species."

Nobody ever named the starling a state bird.

Of course we are momentarily pleased when starlings appear in early spring, harbingers of warmer days even though the snow has just begun to disappear. But they behave badly at the feeder, ganging up to scare off the chickadees and sparrows. Roosting in the maples, their parleys are discordant. Every year a querulous pair nests in the eaves under our bedroom window, waking us with squawks and flitterings, racing back and forth from the barn with long strands of hay for nest making, strewing the excess messily all over the holly bushes beneath, then frantically rushing in and out in day-long feeding of increasingly raucous offspring. And every year one or two will fly in an open window or tumble down the chimney, to beat in panic against door and ceilings, hide in the curtains, spatter over pictures and upholstery, and cause William to climb walls in pursuit, sometimes for half an hour before he can clap a hat over the shivering body and escort it safely outdoors.

To think that starlings were introduced from England in 1897 by some culture-crazed people who had dedicated themselves to importing to the United States every bird mentioned in Shakespeare! And Mozart was so fond of a pet starling — he must have taught it to sing tunefully — that he wrote an epitaph at its death: "A little fool lies here/Whom I held dear,/A starling in the prime/ Of his brief time,/Whose doom it was to drain/Death's bitter pain...He was not naughty, quite,/but gay and bright,/And under all his brag/A foolish wag...And I will lay/That he is now on high/And from the sky/Praises me without pay/In his friendly way..."

If Mozart loved a starling, then they can't be all bad. With a decided effort of will, I invoke St. Francis and try to include them in impartial love of all creatures great and small.

To enter the barn now is to be almost overcome by the concentrated fragrance of newly piled hay. It is of all scents the sweetest and most comforting. It contains the memory of summer's sun-blessed green and the promise of winter's provision. The tiers of bales rise in the loft almost to the highest peak of the gable, where a window frames the swallows' busy traffic. This year there has been such unprecedentedly fine haying weather that we do not go to bed haunted by the fear that wet hay will ferment, heat up to combustion point, and in the middle of the night envelop the barn in the sort of instant conflagration that annually destroys a percentage at this time of harvest. I cannot bear to read of these fires, for so few barns are rebuilt these days. A great old barn in use is a thing of beauty, terribly vulnerable, irreplaceable, very nearly holy.

The fair weather continues. We have had one storm, like a political campaign full of thunderous promises, but only a few drops of needed rain. Chickory, the naive blue of a Wordsworth maiden's eyes, appears at all the roadsides, and tiger lilies flaunt their hot orange caps on country banks and village lanes. In old fields milkweeds spring up to serve as nursery and restaurant to this year's crop of Monarch butterflies. Ferns reach Brobdingnagian proportions in the woods.

There is a great profusion of daisies this year. Saint Augustine of Canterbury taught that "in paradise all righteous souls will be united, like the daisies that grow together in the meadows" — a charming thought, but our meadows are abloom not only with united daisies but also hundreds of thousands of other plants, righteous or not: dogbane with its pale pink bells, striped interior, back-curving petals; white and pink wild spirea, known as steeplebush or hardtack; pale yellow cinquefoil, a flower to embroider on a sampler; Queen Anne's lace spreading handkerchiefs everywhere; chrome-yellow bird's-foot trefoil, called hop-o'-my-thumb and other names associated with the little people; cocky black-eyed Susans not at all particular where they make their home; cow parsnips, five feet or more of outsize leaves and coarse white flowers; golden trefoil, like tiny upside-down bee hives; and purple loosestrife, brought by Puritans from England where it had been cherished in cottage gardens, now spreading all too prolifically over the northeast.

What variety, what largesse, what great fortune to live in these Elysian fields!

After a late lunch, I went out to the garden, having set myself the task of weeding the quadrant where celery, spinach, beets and Swiss chard compete with an army of ragweed, quack grass, purslane and something I can't identify but call simply "manure weed." I spent hour after hour pulling out, heaping up, carting off weeds by their hundreds and thousands, ignoring the ache in my hands that lives beneath the thumbs.

This ache is, the doctor tells me, something called the carpal tunnel syndrome — the nerve running from thumb to wrist pinched by muscle swelling. My home medical encyclopedia says it is an affliction mainly of middle-aged women who overdo gardening and sewing. Sewing I rarely do — with a mother and daughters all expert needlewomen, there's no point in my persisting in my own clumsy stitchery. So that leaves gardening as the probable cause. The cures are a) splinting the hand for as long as it takes to recover; b) operating to reduce the pressure; or c) resting the hand competely for several weeks. None of the above is appealing or possible, so ignoring it seems the best alternative.

Instead of thinking about these particular hands as they yanked and contended with obstinate weeds and shook off the dirt, my mind wandered about on the subject of hands in general. The whole of agriculture is possible only because we have these human hands with their clever opposing thumbs. The other primates might have managed to do something about sowing and harvesting, but they never had to think of it, what with bananas and breadfruit and such literally handy in the milieux they frequent. We did think of it, but it wouldn't have done us any good if we hadn't had these marvelous hands rather than paws. Other animals could scratch a hole in the ground and bury nuts or bones, but only we could pick up a seed between thumb and forefinger and thoughtfully place it in a furrow. And after the patted-down seed had germinated, along with all the surrounding weeds we had learned to recognize as not being useful grain or vegetable, we could take that same thumb and forefinger and pull out the extraneous plants that threatened our crop.

There were more than enough extraneous plants threatening this particular crop to allow plenty of time for ruminating while carrying on half-mindedly the business at hand. I thought of how hands appear in our vocabulary — hand of friendship, second-hand (in terms of both clocks and usage), red-handed, backhanded, hand-me-down, hand in hand, handicapped, deckhand, farmhand, the hand of fate (presumably responsible for the handwriting on the wall). I thought of how we put a hand over the heart to denote loyalty, a hand on the Bible to swear truthfulness, a hand on a shoulder to convey sympathy or on the back for congratulations and encouragement, a hand up to the helpless, a hand to the brow when it is pain or despair, a hand on the head for blessing. Two hands for clapping, two hands for prayer. And of course that ancient anthropomorphism, the hands of God, into which we put our destinies when we can no longer handle them ourselves.

I thought of the hand of Fatma, that symbol seen throughout the Moslem world, painted blue on whitewashed house walls, wrought in silver and hung about the necks of brides, woven into carpet designs — all to bring good fortune from the daughter of Mohammed. In this same Islamic world, thieves, by Koranic law, have their hands cut off.

That brought to mind a contemporary barbarism, the cutting off of the hands of a young girl by the subway train into whose path she had been shoved by a New York mugger of singular depravity. This crime haunted us all, by its rabid cruelty and by the particular tragedy of the girl's having been a gifted musician. It was the incredibly skilled hands of the surgeons, working as a team for some 16 hours, that rejoined the severed hands and saved the girl from the surrogation of prothesis, though she may never play the flute again.

I thought of all the music that is possible — all except vocal — because our hands can finger keys, stop up holes in reeds, draw a bow, bang a drum — everything the four-footed world must do without. And with the alphabet — all those significant squiggles drawn and put together to make words — the hands make possible the transference of thought in ranges infinitely beyond what the voice alone could attempt. Numbers, too, from the clay tablet to the computer.

And it is a hand, a human hand, that would push the final button to leave a world where even the weeds would be radioactive.

A string of matched jewels have been the days of this fortnight. Children and those responsible for weddings, picnics, parades and family reunions have rejoiced to wake morning after morning to sun-filled skies. *Friday: Glorious. Saturday: Glorious* was the forecast in the local paper for the weekend.

But anxiety is deepening throughout the state while crops slow their growth and start to shrivel in fields and gardens. The surface of the soil bleaches and cracks. Each day the water level drops in streams and ponds. The hills remain green, but a film of yellow alters the color scheme in valleys and open spaces. This prolonged period of hot, clear days, with even the usual brief thunderstorms skirting this valley to descend fiercely upon the counties south of our hills, has been a mixed blessing to those who have extensive hayfields; they have enjoyed uninterrupted time to get the hay cut, dried and stored, but the grain has ripened too rapidly, ahead of the reapers, acre upon acre suffused with that purple sheen that means the grass has passed its zenith of perfection and is drying out, going to seed. And where the mowings have been cropped, the new shoots trying to spring up and make a second mowing are stunted and seared. Even the corn, which has grown almost visibly in response to the day-long exhortations of the sun, now begins to flag, the lower leaves paling and drooping. There is talk about declaring some of these valleys disaster areas.

In July of 1901, seven Boston clergymen preached on the topic, "Can Prayer Bring Rain?" Four of them concluded that it could, three had reservations; it is not recorded whether or not they made a field test. This Sunday, the congregation of the local church gathered by the river, as they often do in summer, to hold an outdoor service. There is an altar of hay bales and a cross of two weathered timbers, brought by Justin Alcott in his capacity as deacon in his farm truck and set up with a minimum of ceremony. Folding chairs are put in place for those who prefer to sit in some comfort, though children and young people are likely to settle themselves on the grass. The river has shrunk within its banks, exposing cairns of stone left by the last glacier and pebble-strewn reefs. Beyond, cornfields stretch to the base of the hills. Beneath our feet the grass is dry and brown, and dust billows from the road.

Two children are baptized: a bright-eyed baby in frilly white dress, held first by one and then the other of her young parents; and a girl of seven or eight. The girl's mother stands beside her during the ceremony, a slab of a woman with hair like crows' wings and an impassive Indian face. Her daughter too is dark-haired and bronze-skinned, but her face portrays a full range of emotions — embarrassment, pride, humour, some sense of spiritual occasion, and joy.

The minister dips his finger in a bowl held by a deacon, and dabs the foreheads of the baby and the girl, murmuring the promise of salvation that is the comfort of Christians. The old minister in his black robe used to stand precariously on a rock, reaching down into the rushing waters to bring up the moisture with which he marked the brows of the candidates for baptism. But that was before the flood and the reconstruction of the banks with great alien blocks of marble from the quarry that make dangerous footing. The new minister wears a plaid jacket and is wary of drama.

Later in the service we are asked to name our concerns and those to be held in special prayers. We hear them spoken shyly: Donald Merton, who will undergo surgery this week. Old Mrs. McMichaels, slowly expiring in a nursing home. A student who will be leaving for a year in Africa. The participants in a national church conference. Then, unexpectedly, the victims of floods in the northwestern states. No one speaks up to ask God's mercy of rain upon our own lands. The minister does not pray for rain. Rain is not mentioned at all, though certainly the thought of it clouds the minds of nearly all present. Is this a proud Vermont refusal to petition for help in one's own need, while allowing it for others? Is it a kind of primitive reluctance to attempt to interfere with the workings of nature lest a greater trouble befall? Whatever, no prayers are made for rain this day in this place.

But we go home to watch the sky, and by evening observe the massing of clouds in the west, hearing with a rush of hope the forecast: *Showers possible tomorrow.*

Rain began falling sometime before dawn. We heard its serious tune on the metal roof on awakening, and remembered Saint Swithin:

St. Swithin's day if thou dost rain
For forty days it will remain;
St. Swithin's day if thou be fair,
For forty days 'twill rain na mair.

More than a thousand years ago on this day, the sacred bones of St. Swithin were moved from his self-chosen humble grave to a place of honor in Winchester Cathedral, where he had once served as bishop. The saint's displeasure at this transferral was expressed, so the legend goes, in a violent storm which drenched the procession carrying his disinterred remains where he didn't want them to go. He seems to have been in his lifetime an obstinately good man, inviting the hungry poor to his table rather than the overfed rich, and persuading Aethelwulf, the Anglo-Saxon king who had appointed him bishop, to tithe the royal lands, granting them to the church. When Swithin declared as he was dying that he wished to be buried not within the church but outside in "a poor and unworthy place," he meant what he said and invoked a forty-day downpour to make his point.

Well, whatever the next forty days may bring, it was a grand soaking we were given until late in the afternoon. Elsewhere in the state there were floods, but we were spared such excess. The earth drank in the good moisture, grass greened under its benediction, plants and flowers revived, and the great colonies of leaves living upon every tree could be heard in a murmuring of thankfulness.

In the evening, there was a clearing and a spectacular sunset lighting up not just the west but the whole demi-globe.

In the orchard, the tallest, healthiest, patriarchal tree stood rooted on a slight rise above the rest. Unsprayed and unpruned for the past thirty years, it was unfailingly hardy and prolific. It had been especially beautiful this spring when the rugged branches leafed out in tender green, and white blossoms provided a pavilion for a host of bees. Red-winged blackbirds caroled from its heights, and a family of robins set up housekeeping in a cleft with a view which would have had a real estate agent groping for adjectives. The white petals fell in the swift-growing grass calicoed with buttercups, daisies, and Indian paintbrush. Infinitesimal hard green fruits appeared, the same color as the leaves. The apple tree was once again well along on its season's work, and seemed somehow proud and content in its beauty and usefulness and durability.

The morning after a night of fierce wind, it was found struck down, the gnarled grey trunk split down the middle, the two major lower branches broken off, the raw inner wood splintered and exposed indecently. It was like seeing a happy, active old friend suddenly smitten by a grave injury. The branches lay across the grass, awkward, incongruous green bowers with hundreds of jewel-green apples the size of walnuts clustered in the boughs. It would have been a bounteous crop of those favorite Cortlands that make such memorable pies and delectable sauce.

Perhaps, in the mysterious brave process that old apple trees often manifest, there may be just enough connection left with the roots so that the apples will live and ripen. We shall not cut it down yet. But its life is nearly at an end and we are already in mourning. Small comfort that apple wood gives forth the sweetest fragrance from the winter hearth.

Picking raspberries, on a day blessedly cool after a week of high temperatures, with clouds playing tag all over a bright blue playground, I find only a few berries ripe on each bush, the rest either already eaten by wildlings or still hard white thimbles. So Mr. Mac-Gregor and I wander far afield, searching out promising patches while the berry bucket fills slowly.

We come around the corner of the old sheepbarn with its southward view which is always so friendly in its greeting from meadows, woods and hills. We have put in a new foundation, with an idea of one day restoring the barn, but as of now the south end is missing most of its clapboards, making a capacious high-beamed room open to breezes and sunlight.

As I stand there for a moment contemplatively, the quiet is broken by the sound of something falling on the exposed sill of the barn. I look back, and there on the silvered face of the wood is an odd golden shape about half the size of a tennis ball. I pick it up and study it. The material is spongy and I can see that it is composed of cells something like a honeycomb. Each one is lined with a darker pocket that must have been the protective skin of a wasp in its pupal stage. Now in this cross-section a fragment of a community nursery is revealed, abandoned, but with a residue of papery skins and a sticky liquid.

Where has it come from? Mr. MacGregor's nose points upward. He is standing perfectly still in the long grass and briars just outside the barn threshold, his nose quivering. I follow his stare, and there on the loft beam above is a tiny quivering head with peering dark eyes.

It is a chipmunk, and I see immediately that we have disturbed him at a meal, indeed have caused him to drop it. He edges forward into full view, eyes darting from the treasure I hold in my hand to Mr. MacGregor. How like these two animals are in their tawny color- ings, their boldness, their curiosity, but the one so large, the other so small and neatly made. Mr. MacGregor does not bark as he often does at animals who venture into his territory. He seems to realize that this is the chipmunk's kingdom, and we the intruders. The chip- munk flicks back out of sight, then instantly reappears. He repeats this again and again, like a comic little puppet. The conflict between appetite and fear could not be more vividly manifest.

I hold out the segment of wasp nest, speaking quietly to the chip- munk. *Come. Here it is. We'll not harm you.*

The chipmunk gazes from my face to my hand. He makes a motion to climb down but thinks better of it. We remain for several moments frozen in a tableau of unresolved elements. Then I lay the nest back on the sill where it had first fallen. I move away a few feet into the high grass near the wild cherry tree, Mr. MacGregor at my side. I keep my eye on the chipmunk, but he stays on his high perch, the sleek head moving rapidly from side to side, ears and eyes exquis- itely alert.

Then I spy a raspberry branch with a whole cluster of tender red berries, and give them my whole attention for a moment. When I look back, the chipmunk is not up on his beam. And the wasp nest I'd left below is no longer there. I just glimpse a disappearing tail as the chipmunk scuttles under the fallen foundation stones. He is safe now with his prize.

Come, MacGregor. That was an interesting encounter for us, but we'll leave him in peace. And we make our way through the thick growth of vines, hardtack, nettles and purple nightshade to the open meadow, where by a far wall grows a beckoning mass of raspberry bushes, sure to be laden with fully ripe berries.

A pall of heat lies over the entire northeast. It is 90 degrees in the shade on the north side of the house at 8:00 a.m. The sun is feverish. A heat haze blurs the horizon, and even the forested summits of the hills look wilted. The horses stay within the shadowed barn rather than in pasture sunlight where flies are a constant irritation. We are one with Jane Austen, who in 1796 wrote to her sister, "What dreadful hot weather we have! It keeps me in a continual state of inelegance."

A check of the zucchini patch proves they really do breed in the night, for there are half a dozen new monsters just where I picked every last one yesterday. Flimsy-looking cabbage butterflies flit erratically over the flourishing broccoli, cabbage and cauliflower plants, looking for the most perfect ones in which to lay their horrid little green eggs which will develop into horrid big green worms. These butterflies are maddeningly difficult to catch, fluttering off just before they alight where you await them. One of my garden books recommends chasing them with tennis racquets, but I have enough trouble hitting a ball — I'd never succeed with these flighty pests. In any case it is far too hot to go galloping around the garden in vain pursuit.

Much better to take up the peas that were gathered with dew still on them and repair to the hammock to shell them. This is a pleasant chore, the peas thunking into the pot with a satisfying sound, and no more brain activity required than to wonder why we talk about "like as two peas in a pod" when no pod I have ever examined contained two peas which were identical twins.

Stephanie's little girls have come up from the West Indies for their annual Vermont holiday, delighting in all our northern novelties. They are splendid volunteers in all manner of tasks. Except weeding. *No* one wants to do that for more than five minutes. When I had Natalie beside me pulling out chickweed, ragweed, mullein and dock from the garden the other day, I said something about how perhaps one day when she's grown up she could have a place in the country like this. Natalie, who hasn't a lazy bone in her body, surprised me by saying "No." "Why not?" "Too much work."

Just now Katie has taken all three off berrying. We'd all had fitful sleep last night, and were alarmed by a frightful wild scream from somewhere below the pond at two a.m. Mr. MacGregor had barked frantically for half an hour. At breakfast we speculated on what it might have been, the favorite candidate being the prehistoric Bigfoot.

Now the girls come panting up the hill in great excitement, only a handful of berries in their pails. They can't wait to tell me, calling ahead: "Bears! Bears! We found bear scats in the raspberries! Lots of them, full of seeds! *That's* who was doing the screaming last night!"

The girls shudder and roll their eyes and can't stop talking about it. "What if we'd walked right *into* them?"

I guess it will be a while before anyone ventures into that acre looking for berries again.

The Lions Club has held its yearly auction on the green, taking in over two thousand dollars for worthy causes. Trucks are sent around beforehand and everyone donates something from attic, basement, garage or barn. There are always some nice items, like maple syrup, a handmade butternut table, cartons of books (these usually go for 45 cents a box), or a load of gravel. There are also crippled washing machines, broken lawn mowers, lamps with chewed cords and cracked shades.

Everyone walks around inspecting these articles spread around the bandstand before settling down under the maple and pine trees to enjoy the auctioneer's jokes, chat with relatives, and make an occasional bid. Usually comments about quality are muted, because that battered toaster or croquet set missing a mallet could well have been contributed by a neighbor and everyone wants to avoid hurt feelings. However, this time when a particularly woebegone item of bedding came up for a bid, I heard Philo Ward just behind me mutter to his teenage son, "That's a *mother-in-law* mattress!"

Swallows may be splendid navigators, but they are rather careless about siting their dwellings. On the rafters and beams of our barns, mottled with more than a century of their droppings, swallows construct their nests in absurdly precarious positions. They are perched atop rounded timbers, under window sills, in the cracks between joists, anywhere at all.

One nest just inside the big north doors of the great barn is squeezed into such a constricted space that the infants are crammed into an almost lethal family unity and the parents must perform acrobatic feats each time they arrive with sustenance. Inevitably, one of the babies was shoved-or-pushed out of the nest, and, as the French put it, fell himself to the barn floor. Somehow Katie and Margot discovered him before the cats did, and brought him to the house to be nested in a shoe-box lined with cotton.

The young swallow, a bristly-looking collection of dark new feathers, was bright-eyed, vocal, and apparently healthy. The open maw was his most prominent feature. The girls manfully swatted flies, robbed spider webs, and excavated for worms which they chopped up into junior portions. The fledgling was served every fifteen minutes all day long and responded with excellent appetite. His rescuers were unfeignedly relieved when he at last settled down to sleep at nine o'clock in his box beside Katie's bed. She set her alarm for 4 a.m. to be certain she waked in time for his breakfast.

We heard the muffled note of the alarm in the morning, heard the sounds of her rising, then silence. When there were no further movements from her quarters, we made the obvious surmise.

At breakfast Margot announced quite casually that the baby swallow had "popped off." The girls recognized the odds against successful salvaging of such a young bird and did not protest or grieve when they failed. Nevertheless, as Katie said, "It would have been such a triumph if we could have kept him alive."

"I would have loved teaching him to fly," said Margot.

The Yellow Transparent apples are now so numerous that this tree can only bring to mind the golden apples of Hesperides.

That unexpected plateau set in the midst of all the tilting and rolling of our domain, where the Bartons once, in the interval when Vermont deer were almost exterminated, spread their vegetable garden to the sun, is now a serene stretch of grass, a kind of natural belvedere where one can stand at the edge where it drops off precipitously, looking down on the dell where the pond's eye reflects the shifting colors of heaven, or over the tops of the phalanxes of pine and spruce that stretch down to the valley, or across the familiar outlines of the hills that define our southern horizon and the broken architecture of those to the west guarding the pass to Brandon. Here in this place of specific character like no other in our acres, stands an elm of extraordinary height and symmetry, a single vertical in that open space, its limbs fanning out at the top of the high thrust of trunk into a pattern of such grace and rightness against whatever weather the day is giving us, that I always think of it as "the harp of the meadow." It can be seen from the house, and, when one is lying afloat in the pond, it is there to the east like an agreeable friend, the tallest greenery against the clouds.

This is the one elm that this summer seemed to be responding to the drastic and frighteningly expensive treatment to which we had committed five of the most precious in our care. We could not possibly ward off from every elm on our land the deadly blight which has so relentlessly changed the look of towns, roadsides and farmland as year after year more and more of these magnificent trees have sickened, succumbed, and been chopped down or left as pitiable skeletons. But we were prepared to fight for those five as we would for the health of a threatened member of the family.

And so the crews of tree surgeons have come for two years, with their pruning saws and tanks of antiseptic spray to be injected under the bark where the villainous fungi do their damage. Theirs is a grave dedication to a crusade, but these tree physicians make no promise that their measures will be successful. How could they, when the attackers move so inexorably from the cadavers of elms already slain to the nearest healthy specimen to begin their cruel disemboweling of life juices all over again?

But we had hope — the five we had chosen in the awful business of triage seemed to be holding their own. Each spring we watched anxiously as leaves budded and expanded, searching for the signs of yellowing in a high branch which would mean the disease had gotten a foothold despite preventive measures. It was working, we thought. In May all seemed well, but in June the elm between house and orchard, the two beside the road, the one next the barn, all four were obviously sickening, and so mortally that it would be money thrown away to treat them further. But the one most distant, protected by its isolation, the harp of the meadow, grew green and stately as ever, and gave our hearts consolation in a time of so much loss.

Then on a Sunday afternoon of great heat and air heavy with menace, the sky blackened, thunder cannonaded in the west, and a solid bank of storm clouds moved toward us, shooting out bolts of lightening in a frenzied fusillade. The black clouds were so low, the thunder claps so deafeningly close, the lightning so nearly continuous and coming closer so rapidly, that we in the house knew once again how exposed and helpless we are on our hill.

We closed the windows, of course, and I turned off the water and moved away from the sink where I had been scrubbing vegetables, to go sit quietly in the dining room now dark as night except when lit by angry flashes of lightning which came ominously closer. I looked out at the dove weathervane on the barn bravely flying into the storm, and blessed that lightning rod salesman who long ago had persuaded us to protect barn and house with an array of metal conductors strategically ranged on ridgepoles. Then came an electrical flaring as if Jove himself were going mad astride our roof, the air crackled within the room, the lights went out, and an end-of-the-world crash shook and deafened us.

The house did not go up in flames, nor the barns. We gulped, smiled weakly, rushed to assess damage. Circuits on the south side of the house all out, but no fire, and the great maples stood intact. Then the deluge, a furious lashing and teeming, wild fountains and rivers of water everywhere, the gardens battered and flattened, the earth ravaged and flooded.

It was not until the next morning that we saw where Jove had aimed his bolt. The harp of the meadow still stood. But down its side ran a long jagged wound. The bark had sprung back from the spot on the trunk where the force of the inner explosion had thrust out a splintered mass of heartwood, just below the point where the limbs branch upward. If you had not seen the wound from the other side, you would have thought the tree intact, except for a certain odd stillness about the leafy crown that suggested a state of shock, and a faintly sulphurous tinge to the green of its leaves.

This morning, my brother, who was trained as a forester, walked down to examine the tree. I waited up by the house for his diagnosis, trying to read his expression as he came to the kitchen door. "It's bad," he told me. "But maybe not fatal. It could survive. Give it a year."

We'll give it a year. All the years it needs.

There is only one harp of the meadow.

August is a month for the rest of the world to come to Vermont. On the valley roads and every byway we see young bicyclers pedaling laboriously uphill, flying jubilantly down — hairy lads with bare bronzed torsos, girls with bulging calves and orange knapsacks, bright flags fluttering on long wands from the handlebars to keep the groups together and make them more visible to motorists. From thousands of out-of-state cars tourists pour out to photograph red barns and white steeples. We glance curiously at the license plates, some from great distances — Texas, Alaska, Ultima Thule — and experience an inevitable surge of provincial superiority: Poor things, just visiting. We *live* here.

Mr. MacGregor's barking at the window alerted us. Looking out in the direction his nose pointed, we saw below in the southwest hayfield a party of deer. It was unmistakably a party, for they were frisking and dancing about in a fashion quite unlike their usual wary stance. There were three — four — no, five — no, *eight* of them. The meadow with its backdrop of dense woods and hills defined against a darkening sky formed a perfect amphitheatre, its floor a luxuriant green after the recent rain.

The deer seemed, for once, oblivious to peril, reveling in the openness and sparkling air. Several were yearlings, leaping with a special esprit, circling and feinting in graceful abandon. The others stood on tiptoe, moving in less abandoned fashion but clearly part of the impromptu cotillion. It went on for several moments; how much longer it might have continued we can't know, for a car came noisily up the hill and all the dancers fled, white tails flashing, over the stone wall and into the woods. It was a delight to see this spontaneous performance, for deer lead such endangered lives, constantly on the *qui vive,* that such a moment of sheer carefree rapture must be truly rare.

Maël, who is six, lying on the grass watching the sun go down and the evening star appear: "The moon is the star's mother. His father was a giant star who broke into a trillion pieces and made all those other stars. The sun is waiting for a minute for his mother to come and put him to bed."

Coming home from the village concert we see the whole valley lying under the spell of the full moon riding above the hills. The house gleams white where it is not in deep shadow. In the garden, colors of the flower faces are muted, but discernable under the theatrical moon illumination. We stay out, strolling in the wet grass, the chill in the air negated by the false warmth of the pervasive moonlight.

The familiar outlines of the hills take on another dimension in this radiance, quite a different character from their sunlit selves. There is a sense that the mountains are not at all inert masses, but sentient, alive to the gravitational pull of the imperious moon, all their molecules dancing in place, that it would take only a trifle more lunar seduction to start them moving in sensuous response.

At last we in our light clothing feel the sharp air honing itself on our skin, and we come into the house where lamplight makes a kind of warmth. How the house rings with sound! It is a concert of crickets, coming from every room. The high trilling seems to be everywhere, indeed it is everywhere. The crickets, coming in out of the cold, have possessed themselves of a desirable residence, rent-free, and we are become the intruders. There is no doubt of the meaning — autumn is just over the hills.

Next morning, August fog claims the valley and holds it against the sun's persuasions deep into the day. On the ridgepole of the barn, some twenty swallows perch tentatively. Others arrange themselves on the cardinals of the weathervane, one even sitting on the copper head of Noah's dove. This is a flight lesson, for among the little flock are two or three slightly larger than the rest and clearly tutors. The fledglings ruffle their feathers and can be seen to be reluctant pupils.

One takes off, in a line with the barn roof, straight down into the tall grass below. In a moment he flies back up again, presumably to congratulations. Others take their turns, and though I cannot stay to gauge their progress, surely they do learn, strengthening wings and courage, working toward the confident skill they will need so soon in the impossibly long passage southward.

There will be a morning, not far off, when we look to the barn, will see no swallows there, will hear a sudden silence in the air, see a sudden emptiness in our sky. Swallows do our summer make, and with their going, summer is over. Come September, the only bird silhouetted above the barn will be the weathervane dove, heading into the northwest wind.

Heavy white mists cloak the valley in the mornings. Spiderwebs are revealed in unexpected sites as sunlight catches brilliant drops of dew strung on every line and span — such elegant constructions, lighted with prisms! During the day the temperature climbs and the land swoons under the embrace of the sun. It is the season when solid walls of corn line the roads, and marauding raccoons are flung lifeless on to the pavement by speeding automobiles.

Of course raccoons are not thieves, only clever foragers in their own justifiable behalf, but wasn't it one of Nature's droll tricks to give them bandit masks so like those of human burglars? We have already, despite the electric fence around the garden, found part of a row of corn stripped and partly-eaten cobs lying with broken stalks and leaves. We set the cage-trap, but in the morning it had been sprung and was empty. "Obviously," said William, "there are two of them and they work as a team. One gets caught, the other lets him out."

On his way to the village this morning, coming to the spot where our brook comes out by the road, William saw a pair of well-fed young raccoons emerging on their way to the cornfield on the opposite side. He told me about it when he got home. "I could have run over them quite easily. With dexterous driving, I could have run over one with the left front wheel, one with the right."

He shook his head, half-apologetically, and demanded: "Could *you* have done it?"

Zinnias and marigolds in the garden are the colors of Indian saris, and in the fields goldenrod in countless numbers give a brassy shine to the landscape. The round puce-colored heads of Joe Pye weed crop up in every pasture. Asters begin to appear, all sizes from barely there to grand ebullient bursts, in colors from mouse-pale to Oriental purple.

Elderberries are ripe, and this year we have managed to gather them before they have been all gobbled by birds. The girls and I fill a couple of laundry baskets with the umbels covered with little purple-black beads, then spend an hour or two in the fussy task of separating them from their stems, staining our fingers a fine ruby red. Tomorrow we'll pile the berries in the largest kettle, simmer them, strain the juices, add mounds of sugar, heat until the liquid reaches "a rolling boil which cannot be stirred down," then ladle the jelly into sterlized jars, sealing them with wax. It is a rather pressured performance, with timing of the essence. When it is successfully accomplished, the jelly-makers sit down to admire the rows of stubby glasses gleaming like garnets. We know the tart summer taste of elderberries will give us pleasure all through the white months of winter.

Emma, forced to bring along arithmetic and grammar books from her lycée for summer study, protests: "Counting doesn't make the sunshine yellower, and reading can't make the hills prettier. I just want to draw and paint and be an artist every day of my whole life."

A day of heaviness, humidity, fog, weighted air and circumscribed vision. All the way to Grafton and back, the hills hidden by a wash of thick mist, lakes and ponds glimpsed as fragments of hammered metal. Walking, the level of the sunken clouds seemed just overhead. A pressure on the temples, an aching of the mind.

At night, near midnight, a great wind rising, lightning scribbling its graffiti, thunder rolling closer. Suddenly the house is the center of the storm, ourselves at the heart of the thunder, the lightning, the walls vibrating to its sonorous rage. It is a time we remember that in the average thunderstorm, the released energy is the equivalent of a 20-kiloton atomic bomb. We are once again humbled by reminders of human impotence as nature goes about her business.

The thunder and lashing rain move on, subsiding as far as we are concerned, and we can drift back to sleep.

Next morning, that dazzling clarity of light and sky that follows a clearing-by-storm, a crackling coolness in the air, sharpened vision, wits and tempers running at optimum, every nerve energized by the recharging of the atmosphere.

What can they know of this, who spend their lives behind closed windows, in manufactured evenness of temperature and humidity, under the unwinking glare of fluorescent lights? I do believe humans were meant to be affected by the weather.

We've had three autumnally cool days, with the little girls, accustomed to tropical temperatures, hugging their rib cages and shivering, asking William to light a fire in the dining room and requesting hot water bottles at bedtime.

A cosmopolitan newcomer, picking up her mail, commented on the brisk weather: "It's a typical Mexico City day!"

Our postmaster, who has no small talk, replied: "I'd say it was a Vermont day."

During this month of visitations, we note once again how friends and relatives, especially those coming from the city, alter their tempo once they arrive. Very often they sleep late, appearing for ten o'clock breakfast to tell us, "I had the most amazing dreams last night!" Apparently all the stress and pent impulses of their urban lives explode in extraordinarily vivid dreams once they come to rest here in the quietness. Then they spend hours walking, exploring, or just looking at the view, and even more hours talking. All the events of the month or years since we have last seen them come tumbling out, and we sometimes find ourselves functioning as confessors and therapists.

Some of our guests are genuinely helpful — both males and females can give welcome assistance in cutting down dead trees and stacking firewood, and one friend from Florida declares she likes weeding, it gives her time to think. Others, well-meaning, can only try to lend a hand.

For all of them it is a restorative change of pace. It is an adjustment for us as well, for we must continue to keep up with our chores while alloting large wedges of time for leisurely company meals, prolonged conversations, and later hours than we generally keep. We are happy to share these times with people we love, but there's no denying our routines get disrupted.

These are all too often times for demonstration of William's theory that machines do not care to be taken for granted, and to insure proper appreciation they deliberately collapse at crucial moments when the house is filled with guests — dishwasher, clothes drier, hot water heater — making themselves felt by absence of function.

I perceive that some of our neighbors, especially the working farm families, begin to get a little edgy by the end of August, too many lives thrusting into theirs, too little time for things they *must* do, too keen a sense of summer spinning past without having been sufficiently savored. Mary Morris has put forth the suggestion that the telephone in the booth by the grocery store be put out of order for the rest of the month so there will be no more calls from acquaintances — "Just passing through — thought we'd drop by, we just need directions to get to your place."

Yet I would not go without those rare moments when, after much preparation and discontent with the results, after looking about seeing so much undone and wanting in our domestic arrangements, suddenly I know what old friends are saying about the house and the hills and the envied satisfaction of our life here, and I know that it is all true. I cease making apologies and protests. I relax in contentment, hearing the murmuring of voices on the terrace as the sky melts from sunset to dark and stars appear. For an instant we *are* what we seem to other's eyes, and it is good.

Autumn

My brother Gilbert some time ago, after years of home gardening, sat down and analyzed how much it was costing him. Figuring in his labor with the price of seeds, fertilizer, fencing, watering, canning, freezing, and all the rest, he arrived at a figure of $1.50 per tomato. This was back when $1.50 was worth a good deal more than it is today. Brother gave up gardening, and no doubt for him that made sense. But when I consider what kind of tomato you are going to find in the supermarket — hard as a baseball, the color something from an undertaker's kit, laden with pesticides and hormones, expensively packaged and essentially tasteless, I can only think that $1.50 is perhaps not too much for a sun-riped, juicy, scarlet, tender, chemical-free, gloriously savory homegrown love-apple we feast upon these bounteous September days.

At dusk, looking down from the top curve of the horseshoe road, I see on the topmost branch of a skeletal maple an owl so still and colorless he seems but a slight extension of the limb which is his station. Myself motionless, we stare at one another across a darkening space. His eyes focussing with far more acuity than mine, he can see me with no trouble, but I must strain to make out the pattern of his feathers, the striations almost identical to the design and muted hues of sere leaves and weathered wood. It is a short-eared owl, larger than most, well-fed on the populace of mice, moles, voles and shrews that teems in our undergrowth. His mien is at once haughty and vigilant. He seems part of the twilit landscape, yet one with all the classical associations, from Athena to the early Christian legend that the owl lost its sweet singing voice and fled to the shadows after witnessing the Crucifixion.

I begin to feel uncomfortable in this unblinking presence. Without warning he takes flight, the wings spread in perfect fans. Down the windless air, mothlike, he dips and swerves, landing a thousand feet away on another exposed branch. He is still visible to me from the narrow road above, and I to him. But his flight has been a suggestion that it would be discourteous of me to remain. Courteously, I withdraw. It is an encounter that lasts only a long few moments, totally silent, but somehow charged with significance.

Zinnias and marigolds still riot in the garden, but when they are cut and brought in the house they soon tire and curl their petals. Nevertheless, it is one of the joys of this season to have bowls of them everywhere, the magnificent colors all put together devil-may-care with no need for arrangement. I look at each flower as I strip it of leaves and place it in water, each one a marvel of design and color, no two alike. What God hath wrought!

A bleak pouring down of rain, all day, all night, increasing in intensity at intervals. The house filled with gloomy shadows, pungent with damp-fur smells of dogs. Cats curled in corners. Windowpanes streaming, streaming. The world beyond a grey and questionable foreshortened space.

But how preferable to the hurricanes that yesterday struck the islands off the east coast! We have only to think of the still-visible ravages of the September hurricane of 1938, which even here inland sheared off scores of sugar maples on our hill. Those rows of blackened stumps of trees that once provided syrup year after year have for long been nothing but a cemetery of what had been a splendid grove.

This rain has none of the killing power of a hurricane. Mere rain the woodlands and we can well endure.

Barbara, coming from London on her first visit here, cried out as we drove up to the house, "Good heavens, look at those thistles! In England, you'd be arrested for harboring such things on your property."

It's understandable that in a nation where space is precious, where gardens are regarded reverentially, and where the public weal is maintained by well-understood and generally obeyed regulations, one man's unrestrained crop of thistles could easily be counted not merely un-neighborly but downright criminal. Nothing looks more fragile and aimless than a bit of thistledown floating against an autumnal sky, but nothing could be more purposeful. If it were not for the competition — mulleins, dock, milkweed — thistles might very well take over the earth. We do try to keep them down within a reasonable circumference of house and garden, but if they are not all dug up when infants they spring into triumphant maturity while our backs are turned.

Yet thistles have a place in the chain of being. Naturalist Michael Gordon points out that though at first glance a thistle, closely inspected, may seem swarming with chaotic insect activity, "a megalopolis of disorganized prosperity, crime in the streets, indiscriminate public fornication," it becomes clear that what goes on within its protective corona is an orderly process with no waste as it is visited by ants, flies, snails, grasshoppers, and a procession of pollen-bearing bugs, bees, moths, butterflies and hummingbirds.

Like every other non-toxic plant, thistles used to be boiled up into an infusion to sooth sore throats; Saint Blaise, patron saint of those who suffer from throat ailments, is represented by a thistle. It was also, according to the ancient medical doctrine of like healing like, a cure for a stitch in the side.

And of course the thistle is the emblem of the royal house of Scotland, in commemoration of an unsuccessful 8th-century attack by the

Danes on Stirling Castle. The invaders' presence was revealed when their barefooted scouts clumsily trod upon thistles and let out howls of anguish. The alarm was given and the Scots leapt up to fall upon their enemies, "defeating them with a great slaughter." With the victorious thistle emblem was adopted the motto, *Nemo me impune lacessit,* which, being translated with a burr, comes out "Naebody touches me without rrrregrretting it."

With all its prickliness and persistence, a thistle can be perversely handsome with its lavender and purple flowers atop its tall stalks. To see the golden finches circling about a candelabra of flowering thistle, darting into the blossoms to snatch out the seeds, weaving patterns against a pure blue sky, is to be spectator at one of September's most artful presentations of color, motion, and ecological harmony.

The grapes planted by the Bartons along the pasture wall continue to bear, and today we plucked them. They lie in the cauldron in purple mounds. It seems a pity to crush them, but we do, the royal blood spurting under the pestle. They simmer briefly on the stove, then are spooned into jelly bags. From their ignominious suspension the juice flows rapidly at first, slows to a gentle trickle, then to an exhausted rhythm of single drops. One thinks of Marat in his bathtub, though he was hardly royal. We taste the ichor, and it is headily piquant. This is meant for wine, not to be jelled and jarred and spread on bread. But we have only two gallons of juice, hardly enough to set up a distillery.

It will have to be jelly, with apologies to Bacchus.

Three squirrels on the stone wall beyond the kitchen door. Two sitting upright, tails arched, still as carved figures, one facing the wind, the other backed into it. The third in frenetic motion, zipping between wall and maple tree, snatching up seeds, cupping his little paws in the gesture of a communicant, jaws quivering with nervous haste, eyes darting, tail vibrant, back and forth, back and forth he races. Are the two wall-perchers serving as guards for the third while he fills his belly? Do they take turns? They are identical, their coloring rust and grey and white, their heads beautifully molded, their eyes button-bright. They are, in a word, adorable in the human view even with the knowledge that they are enormously destructive.

We cannot discern any differences, even through binoculars, in the size, shape or sex of this trio. Naturally, we speculate. Father, mother, daughter/son? Husband, wife, mistress? Wife, husband, lover? Siblings? Three brothers? Three sisters? Just friends? The possible combinations are intriguing to the anthropomorphic mind. William's view is that squirrels are at least as inventive in their relationships as human beings, and as careless.

John Burroughs says in *Signs and Seasons,* "If you wish the birds to breed and thrive in your orchard groves, kill every red squirrel that infests the place." Squirrels have had a dubious reputation for ages: in the mythological Norse world-tree, squirrels ran up and down the trunk and branches, stirring discord between heaven and hell.

For all their intriguing qualities, we have determined that we must try to remove them from the premises before winter comes and they monopolize the bird feeders.

Firmly, I put peanuts on the grocery list to be used as bait.

The foreground is in the process of changing its costume from green to motley. Bracken is bronzing, milkweed is glowing with an astonishing impudent yellow, thousands of them now individually visible in fields and pastures, each one calling out, "Look at me! Look at me!" Soon they will be lost in the great mantle of varicolors that will robe the land.

Three houses having been broken into, the furnishings having been loaded onto trucks to be transported out of state to reappear in antique shops hundreds of miles away, people have been told by the state trooper to keep their doors locked. It doesn't come easy, the habit of locking up, the habit of distrust. Says Lawrence Woods, "Used to be, you had a collie dog on the doorstep to tell you if you had company. Anybody came and knocked on the door, if there was nobody home, they'd go away. Now you've got to sit on that doorstep yourself with a rifle crosst your knee. Changing times."

The swallows have flown, leaving our sky the poorer without their daylong swoopings and aerial acrobatics. But this morning a dead swallow was found at the kitchen door, perfect, no sign of injury. He may have been a straggler from farther north who flew full tilt into the glass door, dying instantly of concussion.

He is beautiful, the indigo, buff and white one of those artful combinations of coloring in which nature delights. The wings, which were to have borne him to the Caribbean and perhaps as far as Argentina, are a marvel of construction, tiers of shapely feathers graduating in perfect precision. No wonder we give wings to our semi-divinities, no wonder those Italian artists vied in painting the glorious wings of angels. There is perhaps nothing so mysterious to us earthbound humans.

I remember a painting in the Toronto Art Museum, Icarus wearing the wings devised by Daedalus, the father at his son's shoulder speaking a word of encouragement, the youth listening, gazing outward with an expression of mingled trust and fear. While I studied the painting, a plump woman, surely an amateur guide, came along with a straggle of tourists. They paused momentarily and I stepped back to give them a better view. "That's a picture of a boy who wants to fly and his father who's telling him not to," the woman said. No one contradicted her. The tourists gawked dutifully and were moved on briskly. The whole ageless fascination with flight so strongly symbolized by this painting and the legend — a heartbreaker, one which parallels the poignancy of the story of Abraham and Isaac — was lost upon these viewers.

I hold the lifeless swallow and consider for a moment digging a small grave — if he cannot climb the heavens, he ought at least to go to good earth. But it is a busy morning, and the trash collector will be coming shortly. I take the little corpse, wrap it in newspaper, and put it in the garbage can, the one with the top that stays put firmly.

At least the cats won't get him.

The zucchini still proliferate like so many rabbits. The colors vary without much reason that I can guess, some streaked in the manner of verde antique marble, some with green and white awning stripes, the youngest and tenderest dappled like frog legs, the oldest a dead hard green so dark they seem to have been blackened in some nether fires.

There is nothing so nude as a freshly dug, freshly washed potato, its skin faintly colored and so thin as to be almost non-existent. But how hearty are the colors of the tomatoes, once they decide to ripen! What silken skins they have, gleaming scarlet and vermilion, swelling flesh mimicking cheeks and buttocks and bosoms.

Beans, planted three and a half months ago as fat little individual seeds, grow almost as tall as the sunflowers. A robust configuration of leaves climbs up and beyond the poles, tendrils reaching into the air, clusters of pods in all stages of growth from green nail-paring beginnings to upholstered giants not picked soon enough, and masses of creamy blossoms still flowering in ignorance of frosts just over the hill.

The sunflowers have given up gazing heavenward and droop with downcast heads. They have presided jovially over the garden all summer, growing taller and taller. But now that it is a scene of desiccated stalks and senile weeds, the sunflowers seem not to want to look upon it longer, and avert their heads. The birds have already rifled a portion of the seeds and the petals have lost some of their flare, yet a sunflower with its round center, marvelous geometric arrangement of seeds, and circling golden rays still serves as a metaphor for the sun itself, as it has since prehistoric times in every form of art. No wonder it is the flower associated with Saint John the Evangelist, who preached the coming of "The Light of the World."

I put off decapitating them and the job of spreading out their disks to dry in the honey-colored air. The seeds will fuel the hardy flocks whose numbers increase at the feeders as the sun's arc diminishes, but I shall save a handful for planting next year when Phoebus will be back to call them upward again.

After 36 hours of driving rain, the air clears, the mountains return to our ken, and the faded grass is suddenly as green as if it were growing toward May, not October. But in the purged atmosphere, small patches of leaves signal in warning colors, a streak of scarlet in the maples' crests, a yellowing edge to the poplars. The human response is a pang of dismay: Too soon! Too soon! We are not ready. The summer has betrayed us by stealthy withdrawal. So much planned and unaccomplished for the growing season, so little readiness for the season of shutting down and the long night of ice.

William out early one morning in repsonse to two great principles: The Grass Is Greener on the Other Side of the Fence, and Undesirable Citizens Must Be Deported. The first because Gallagher had discovered a breachable section of the pasture fence and had eaten his way right up to the front door, leaving deep hoofprints on the lawn. He was so sated with chlorophyll that it was no task to fling a halter over his monumental neck and lead him back to the barn. Discovering the escape hatch in the pasture fence was not so easy; that meant walking the length of wires strung along lines of tipsy fenceposts that are the pasture's boundaries, doing minor mending all the way as well as major when the point of exit was found.

As for the undesirable citizen, it was one of our squirrel triad who had been lured by a scattering of peanuts into a trap set by the wall under the bird feeder he had so often and so brazenly robbed. It was a trap designed only to hold, not to harm, but the squirrel was naturally terrified to find himself imprisoned, and ran back and forth frantically within the wire confines.

We held the cage and looked at him more closely than had ever been possible in his days of swift-moving freedom, admiring his glossy brindled coat, his amazingly long and efficient clawed toes, his bristling tail, his brilliant dark eyes ringed with white fur giving him an air at once defenseless and dashing. If only he were not so destructive! But at the thought of the girdled roots of the rose bushes, the tulip bulbs providing sustenance for an entire squirrel family last winter and which I am about to replace, not to mention the birds of all feathers who had not the courage to fight for seed against those greedy, bullying creatures, we hardened our hearts and William carried him off, driving across two bends in the river and releasing him in the red pines of the National Forest.

Clarence Worth, our retired pharmacist, laughed when we told him about it. Squirrels, he said, have been known to travel a hundred miles to return to their nests. If this be true, our case may be hopeless.

One of the joys of autumn is the garnering of windfalls in the orchard, especially this year of abundant bearing. The concealing grass hides bushels of apples, easier to reach than those high on the boughs but necessitating a certain amount of stooping and searching. It is a mistake ever to go to the orchard without a container of some sort, for invariably I find myself picking up more than a handful, more than a pocketful, or a jacketful. At the very least, a bushel basket or a large pail should be carried along. It is helpful to take along a child of the proper age, something under ten, and a dog or two can be a congenial though not absolutely necessary accompaniment.

The daily visit to the orchard is a lesson in ecology. The cycle of fruition-decomposition-fertilization takes place right before one's eyes. Only so many apples are fit for gathering; the rest decay and build up the soil around the gnarled roots. It is also a lesson in sharing, for the fruit goes to nourish a world of wild creatures as well as ourselves. You can see the ants, slugs and wasps feasting greedily. The other diners are invisible, but have left their teethmarks everywhere. Woodchucks and deer have a taste for quality, preferring the plumpest, ripest, reddest ones of all, and they do not bother to tidy up after a meal.

This largesse has gone on since August, beginning with the early greenings and yellow transparents. The generous-cheeked Gravensteins, with their shiny pink-striped skins, have had their day, quickly consumed, for their beauty is perishable. Then the meaty Cortlands — even the riven tree has managed a surprising number of fruits — and the Rome Beauties, excellent for pie fillings and Brown Betty pudding.

Now the MacIntosh and Northern Spies are coming on with their scarlet coats and crisp flavor. The Russets still ripen slowly, keeping long after frost.

Some of the trees have nearly given up, their fruit meager, wizened and sour. Even the best produce apples with spots and imperfections. Preparing them for cooking reveals how much must be cut away and discarded. But what heavenly pies they do make, what incomparable applesauce! They are simply not to be compared with the plastic-bagged artificial perfection of the supermarket offerings.

A few of the varieties here are so old-fashioned that no one now remembers what they were once called. Maybe that one is a Bethel apple, suggests an old-timer, or a Bellflower. Might be, but can't say for sure. The most aged tree in the orchard we know is a Baldwin. One night last winter, deep in snow, its massive lichened trunk cracked. Now its branches spread in opposite directions on the ground. Bowed but undefeated, every twig and branch blossomed in May, and now is laden, as it has not been for years, with a bumper crop of firm, perfectly shaped apples, ready to be barreled for the coming winter. There is a lesson here, too, on the possibilities of triumph over disaster. What a noble legacy was left us by every countryman who planted an apple tree!

For some time now the vegetable garden has looked increasingly disheveled as we bring in crops, dig up potatoes, pile up stalks and vines at ends of rows. But most unsightly of all are the tomato trellises, draped with an assortment of protective covers that would be an embarrassment if everyone else hadn't the same sort of collection in view in their gardens. A large vinyl tablecloth, with a pattern of stains. A frayed corduroy bathrobe with broken zipper. A set of kitchen curtains from 1954. A camp blanket with gaping holes. A bathroom rug the cats had ruined. All these have been held down with strings and stakes since the day the radio forecast was for "temperatures in the low thirties tonight." During the day, when it is warm enough, these safeguards have to be peeled back in the hope that the sun will hasten the ripening of the slow-pokes. The tomatoes, suspended from vines now brittle amidst curled dry leaves, are inspected daily, and those sufficiently ripe and not too mutilated by slugs are brought in. A continuous processing goes on — stewed tomatoes, tomato soup, tomato sauce, tomato catsup, just as I had envisioned in April.

When we hear the forecast of "temperatures may drop into the twenties tonight," we give up, pile the remaining tomatoes in laundry baskets, fold up the coverings and take down the trellises. When I get around to sorting them, they are found to be of a variousness — hard green, pale soft green, pinkening, red ripe, rotten. The best are wrapped in tissue paper and put into cartons in the root cellar — they may keep as late as mid-December. The odd-shaped smaller green globes are ranged along window sills to ripen in public, and they must be checked every day for they have a tendency to collapse into evil little heaps. The rest are cooked up, mainly as a base for a soup into which go bits of everything else that happens to come into the kitchen, soups that will be the mainstay of our midday meals all winter long and, if I count aright, into next June when the garden will once again begin to offer its bounty.

At our doorstep, of the two sarvis trees one stands unconcernedly green, the other is tipped with gilt, each leaf outlined as if that greedy king with the golden touch had negligently waved a hand in its direction. Last night he came back to correct his oversight — today the tree is entirely golden.

The early mist lingers now until ten o'clock or so. I think of the valley dwellers going about their business in cotton wool. Up here the shifting veils conceal or tentatively reveal oddly softened shapes and hues. The top half of the yellowing cottonwood tree appears momentarily, then vanishes. Strident hues are muted to whispers. When the fog lifts, finally, after a heavy last muffling of the river bed, the air is still hazed over, the distant hills slightly blurred. But in the foreground, close at hand, there are myriad brightnesses. How handsome are all the vines, Virginia creeper everywhere hanging out its crimson banners, clematis decked with the fluffs of "old man's beard," nightshade ornamented with rubies, bittersweet hung with parti-colored globes.

Every autumn there comes The Harvest Day. It is unscheduled, arriving when the first serious warnings of "hard frost" persuade us to gather in. This year, as always, it came too early for us. There was stinging cold rain with intervals of cranky sunlight. We picked bushels of chard, baskets of beans, the last of the ears of corn. We probed beneath the still-rank leaves for hidden acorn squash. We took more baskets to the orchard, shoes squishing on windfalls, climbed ladders and thrust the long-poled apple-pickers to the high branches. At dusk we brought it all under cover, some in the shed, some in the back corridor, some in pantry and kitchen.

It seems an overwhelming accumulation. The squash in their homely shapes and colors from jade to topaz are the least demanding, requiring nothing more for the moment than ranging on benches and tables, but so much else cries out for processing, the sooner the better. The kitchen is a fine confusion of produce piled on every surface. All pots and vessels are in service, all stove burners working away as we stay up until midnight doing what can't be postponed. The freezers are filling rapidly, we are running out of containers and jars. Thank God the apples can wait.

Right up to the night of the true frost, the marigolds and zinnias rejoiced in eye-popping colors, whole regiments holding up their heads in sectors of the vegetable garden. The morning after the temperature fell below the survival point, it was a grievous spectacle. Nothing but blackened forms and twisted heads, a mass catastrophe irresistibly suggestive of pestilence and holocaust in some hideous chapter of human history, or to come.

In late September, walking uphill at midnight, no longer accompanied by the winking signals of fireflies, our way is faintly illuminated by glowworms. In the low grass by the roadside, their random glimmers are strewn like ghostly flowers. There is something otherworldly about them, netherworldly, as if they emerged at night from graveyards to light the way for hobgoblins. Theirs is a cold and greenish glow, not meant for us. We shiver a little, though the night is mild, and look up at the diamond stars. Theirs is an otherworldly light, but of a clarity and a purity surpassing any we earthlings know. Were we more humble, we might think the light of our human intelligence like that of the glowworms, an infinitesimal flicker, hardly to be seen in the starry blaze of eternity.

At this time of year, we eat like royalty, or like peasants. Potatoes, forked up with the soil clinging to their stone-shapes, scrubbed, baked in their skins to a white mealy consistency, served with dollops of sweet butter. Tomatoes, ripened at the window to a juice-rich pointsettia color, sliced and sprinkled with the Irish-green of minced chives. Carrots pulled from the cooling earth, washed, steamed *al dente,* glazed with butter and a dash of maple syrup. Acorn squash, hollowed out and baked with a stuffing of country sausage. Pumpkins, cut up, cooked with eggs, cream, honey and spices to fill crisp pie crusts. Onions, still with a garden tang at their hearts. Cabbages, chopped into slaw or sliced fine to be added to the last leaves of lettuce. Beans, dried on the vine, now baked long hours with tomato sauce and molasses, or simmered with a hambone into a potage so thick the long-handled wooden spoon stands upright in its depths. Hearty harvest soups, concocted of odds and ends of every vegetable, sometimes with the added richness of broths of chicken or lamb and pearls of barley. And apples — in sauce, served still warm from hours of slow cooking, in pies, or baked so that the rosy skin begins to fall away from the rosy flesh beneath.

Simple food, healthful food, and utterly delicious. Later, we will live on the provisions stored in freezer, jars, and root cellar, all good and nourishing too, but at a remove from this autumnal freshness and ripeness which is the crown of the gardening season.

Going down our hill, slowly, we revel once more in that evanescent interval when each autumn the roadside maples burst into color. They seem to darken their trunks, the better to contrast with their coronas of yellow and orange. The clouds of leaves hold their own light whatever the weather, but to pass beneath them with the sun directly upon them or filtering through the boughs is to have one's soul lit up by a maximum of illumination.

Only a few years ago, this was a passage even more splendid; that was before the death of the oldest maples and the elms. But beyond the line of veterans that remain, in the neglected pastures, strong new young maples have sprung up, their flags of shining leaves rising taller each year, making a promise of grandeur to come.

Rain, two days of it, torrential, ferocious rain. Flooding in the south again. Intervals of impenetrable fog. To think of that limited engagement of fall color going on unseen in this wretched weather! But today the rain grudgingly diminishes and withdraws. By afternoon, we can see how the foliage has advanced.

Coming home from Strafford, down the back roads, along the bold high span of the Interstate, back to the two-lane route that winds through the valley, everywhere the vistas left one dizzy with their fresh-washed color. In the open spaces, ranges of hills were bewitched by color into presenting entirely new perspectives, denying their summer or winter selves. Along the river, swollen now, steel grey and raging white, such a succession of vignettes, each perfect in its composition of tree shapes, water, rocks, that the mind clicked away endlessly, in an attempt to record all of them in a mental album. Impossible. The contrast of green-going gold with full-fledged oranges, ochres, salmon rose, and all the variations of carnival red with the severe immutability of the evergreen answers some basic need for balance in the spectrum. It is satisfying and yet exhilarating in a manner no other season can match.

Crossing the river, making my way up Barton hill through the woods to the point where the clearings begin, a sudden unobstructed perspective of the entire upper slope telegraphs the message: *This* is the most beautiful place of all. Truly the sweeps of color here have an intensity and clarity beyond all the rest seen that day. Perhaps it is because there are so many hardwoods here, such concentrations of maples — sugar, rock, swamp — by the hundreds, that the effect in this prime moment is so stunning. I feel a certain illogical pride in "our" hill's exhibition, and also the recurrent gratitude for the privilege of living here.

It is official. The forester declares that the foliage is at its "peak coloration" in our area, a week early. There are the usual amateur explanations, delivered with authority. It was too dry this summer. Too wet. Too cold. Too hot. They all have merit — all these criticisms of the past season are valid. Whatever, it is true that today we are more magnificent than yesterday, and it is not possible to imagine more magnificence tomorrow.

Such a crop of onions! They have been lying out in rows, "papering over," and now I take a wheelbarrow load of them to a grassy spot where they can be sorted. A few, already sprouting, will go into a Provencal soup. Some of them, still showing signs of moisture, are spread on chicken wire in the warm dry upper room of the small shed. This is a place I love, always quite dusty and with a permanent colony of what Vermonters call "cluster flies" crawling about the unwashed window panes. But the window is southerly, sun pours in, lighting up the corners where the flower pots and seed flats are stacked with all the other gardening paraphernalia, and a few oddments like a half-dozen of the original shutters from the house, still in quite good shape and faded to a grey blue, the color of an April sky.

There is a large opening on the far side leading into the adjoining, larger shed, which, in the mysterious custom of the country, does not actually unite with the small one — there is about a foot of space between the two buildings. At one time they leaned so close together in their lonely age that they virtually became one, but then we arrived and leveled them up and restored their roofing and painted them red. Now there is that ridiculous 12-inch space which must be stepped over to pass between one building and the other.

The larger shed was once used for drying hops. Now its lower section garages three vehicles and the upper contains a trove of old hand-hewn planks, rolls of light fencing, a child-size brass bed, a Christmas angel. I do not need to enter there often. My domain is the smaller, sunny upper room next door to it.

Today from nails protruding from the beams I hang braids of onions, orbs of purple, white, and yellow. They will be safe here until the hard cold sets in.

Down below, at the foot of the rickety stairs, the yellow monster, the tractor with the snow plow, sits and waits.

We keep watch over the guardian maples of the house, the three to the south and three to the north, comparing their shifts of color, one with the other and with the memories of other autumns. As their leaves drift down, each day finds our interiors perceptibly more filled with light. We proceed from the green aqueous air that fills our summer rooms when the maples are in full leaf, to the Florentine light of autumn, to the white clarity of winter light when nothing comes between our windows and the sky but a naked intricacy of branches.

These trees are so much part of the character of the house, inside and out, that it is impossible to imagine our world without them. The youngest one Henley Barton remembers seeing planted in his boyhood seventy years ago — "wasn't bigger around than my wrist then" — and the others were put in a generation or so earlier. How can one be grateful enough for the thought that placed them where they have rooted and flourished? Gideon Barton, his sons and grandsons, spent their lives cutting down trees, moving the forest back farther each year to extend their fields and pastures. It must have marked a turning point when one of them at last actually planted a tree on the cleared ground. Probably it was one of the wives who yearned for summer shade and suggested moving a maple sapling from the woods to stand near the house. However it came about, here stand today five guardians of the house, more precious every year.

The back hall, unheated, has become a way station for produce that will go to the root cellar or be processed later rather than sooner, and some of it to spend the winter here. Baskets, boxes, crocks, pails overflow with redolent harvest — squash, pumpkins, ornamental gourds, cabbages green and purple, glossy green and red peppers. A few pots of straggly geraniums. Beets. Apples, sending out an aroma strong enough to make one tipsy. It is a grand thing for the senses to stand in the midst of all this, and a most reassuring spectacle on the eve of a northern winter. "Oh, it's like Badger's Hall!" exclaimed Bartholomew when he first saw it. And friends who had been living in Asia said, "No wonder Americans celebrate Thanksgiving."

The air mild, a pensive stillness lies over all. The colors are undeniably less brilliant today, a further loss of leaves visible in the upper reaches of the hills. One wants to put out a hand and cry out, "Stay! Stay! You needn't leave so soon! The party isn't over!" Ever present in the mind's eye is the next scene, inexorably approaching, the utter contrast between all this opulence and the relative penury of color to come. It is impossible not to identify it with the human condition, the stripping away of treasures, the onset of age, the inevitability of death.

Late gifts from the garden — reactivated broccoli, little green marbles clinging to stalks of brussels sprouts, gross turnips and rutabagas, some durable ruby-veined Swiss chard that defied the chill, carrots of course, cheerful parsley, and even a few small hidden tomatoes escaped from frost. These are gathered with more appreciation than in the midst of harvest-time when the cascades of vegetables overwhelm us with all-at-onceness. This more leisurely segment of time has rewards, minor in comparison, but welcome too.

The Vermont Cranberry beans, nestled in their pods once handsome green stippled with rose, now crackling brown with a silver lining, resemble birds' eggs so strikingly that one can only smile at Nature's love of visual puns. The perfectly smooth surface, the rounded shape, the pale shine, the speckles of rusty red — how like a thrush's eggs! Of course they are eggs of a kind — seeds encasing embryo plants which could mature into rampant vines festooned with a whole new generation of beans. Thrush eggs — Vermont Cranberry Beans — all containing life, containing the secret of reproduction.

But these beans, falling rhythmically into a bowl as I thumb out the pods that are cast into an untidy pile at my feet, will not come to new life, to reproduction. They are destined for our winter soups, casseroles, stews. I would not eat a thrush's egg. But I certainly intend to eat these beans. When they are cooked, they change color, lose sheen, turn a humble brownish grey not in the least suggestive any longer of porcelain-shelled eggs in a nest. Their anima vitae vanishes in the cooking pot, the life they sustain no longer theirs but ours.

Reasons for melancholy:

The killing frost earlier this year than last, stirring doom fears of ever-shorter growing seasons.

A friend, suddenly looking ten years older, going to the hospital for diagnostic tests.

Confirmation of the rumour that the Merediths-by-the-bridge are selling their family farm to an Arab buyer.

Where the field corn has been cut, the stubbled acres lie striped and patterned in the manner of homespun tweeds. Where the stalks still stand, they seem armies vanquished and leaderless, spectral and shivering. Yet these pale regiments are everywhere surrounded by hayfields reviving after their last cutting into the most vivid vernal green.

The sharp rustiness of bracken climbs up the clearings, echoing the changing garments of the oaks. Our hill is barer than most, those stands of maple swept clean by wind and rain in the upper reaches. The trees however do not seem naked yet. There is a soft greyness enveloping them so that they make smoky patches amid the embers of those still holding their leaves. The birches reveal their special bodily graces and unique whiteness now. Alders, willows, poplars still tremble in their modest greenery-yellerys, and though the cottonwood has turned a gleaming gold, the leaves strewn at her feet are silver and round as old dollars.

On the woodland road over in North Hollow, we are all at once translated into another time, another dimension — a Jacobean scene embroidered in late autumnal colors, each leaf and branch rendered in minute detail but the whole a muted tapestry. Within this composition, with its mustards and olive greens and russets, we spy the figure and the colors for which the background had been stitched — a youth, his hair black as a hawk's feathers, his shirt a pure scarlet, rifle over his shoulder, and, hanging from his left hand, a dead partridge, one wing, striped sepia and white, spread downward into a perfect fan.

For a long moment we are spellbound, viewers of an antique piece of art. Then the boy moves toward a little rise in the road, the partridge swinging in his grasp, the multicolored leaves stirring under his boots. He disappears beyond the borders of the tapestry.

The spell is broken, but the picture remains in the museum of memory.

Indian corn in a triad is hung from the front door to commemorate the harvest — one gold, one russet, one Phoenician purple, the pale husks spread in a fan above the brass knocker. How ancient is this symbol — an offering of thanksgiving to the god of grain for this year's bounty, a magic to conjure fertility in the year to come. It is a reminder, each time we enter the house, of our human dependence on the mystery of seed and growth.

But we are not alone in our pleasure in this emblem of the season's yield. I note with some puzzlement that a few of the glossy yellow kernels are missing. Next day, more of the cob is exposed in its sere geometry. Then there are inroads in the other ears of corn, first the russet, now the purple.

Is it a bird, a squirrel, a chipmunk? How is it done, when is it done? No thief is ever visible when we are near. Yet each day the ears of corn are further ravaged.

Today they hang stripped and skeletal, all color and promise vanished. But someone, something, has been nurtured. Life, doing what it will with our symbol, goes on.

Stacking paper-swathed apples in compartmented boxes to lay away in the root cellar, I am minded of the story, a true story, of the Quaker orchardist. This Friend, whose apple trees had been tended by generations of his family, was progressive enough to invest in a modern temperature-control system for the building where the crated apples were stored. But he was enough of an old-fashioned Quaker to eschew all business on First Day (Sunday), which he devoted entirely to spiritual matters.

The new machinery kept his apples in excellent condition, but he began to be troubled about its working seven days a week. For a long time he wrestled with this problem of scrupulosity. He began to have trouble sleeping, hearing in his mind the hum of that machine as it labored around the clock, day in and day out.

At last, having lain awake most of the night of a Seventh Day and into the early hours of First Day, he rose from his bed, went out to the storage building, and turned off the motor. His soul at ease, he did not turn it on again until the beginning of Second Day. And this he did once a week faithfully from that time on.

The Friend's apples, which had always been of fine quality, now seemed to keep indefinitely in a state of perfection. The new schedule suited their respiratory requirements precisely. As a result, his business has prospered exceedingly.

"Apples," he observes, "like thee and me, keep best with six days on and one day off."

The lushness of new grass is an unseasonable green where every other form of plant life is in a visible state of retirement or decay. The horses, already fattened on thousands of windfalls from the apple trees bordering the pasture, crop the fresh grass with greedy gusto. Their coats are plusher by the day, their rounded torsos storing up brawn against the day when this postscript of grass disappears beneath the snow.

Today October gives us the sky we identify with this month, a sky seamless in its high metallic plating, a burnished blue. It is a day to spring merrily to tasks which are made by its blue brilliance no longer the melancholy grave-diggings of dead summer but the proper clearing away of debris and the making of arrangements for the next act in an ongoing drama.

It is a day to harrow the vegetable garden, digging under all the remnants of a thousand plants we knew and nourished and called by name, but also the masses of weeds which gave us such troubles. At the end of William's labors, the garden space is nearly as neat as in its virginal days of spring. We look at it and envision what an improvement next year's planting will be in every way.

It is a day too for yanking our marigolds, petunias, and such bygone faithfuls, cutting back the phlox and astilbe that bloomed so superbly in their season, spading up the soil and planting bulbs in the perennial beds. Most bulbs do not hint, in shape or color, of what they will produce, but tulips, with their satin skins and sculptured forms, are an exception. Daffodil bulbs can be quite toadlike, knobby and hard, sometimes with several infants splitting off grotesquely. The hairy little buttons of crocus are easier to plant than the tiny wrinkled dung-colored anemones, which have to be examined carefully to distinguish up from down. Hyacinths are gross as thick-necked dowagers.

Whichever is to be planted, there is scarcely a gardening pleasure to match the neat removal of a packet of soil by the metal bulb planter, the sprinkling in at the base of the excavation a benison of bonemeal, the setting in place of the exact bulb chosen for that spot, the replacement of the dirt, the final pressing down of the soil. Moving along on one's knees, constantly removing pebbles and stones to ensure a more comfortable cradle, tearing out the intrusive roots of weeds, trying to keep the bulbs in proper relationships of size, quantity, and color — through all this the mind's eye rejoices in a picture of what will burst forth here within six months time.

Bared, most trees appear shrunken. In summer clothing, a tree's bones are scarcely visible, there is an impression only of luxuriant bulk and density. How deceptive this is becomes apparent, sometimes shockingly, in this season of elimination. There is a maple at the foot of the hill that is a noble landmark in summer, voluminous and rich, and in autumn, a great cumulus of saffron. But now it is revealed as misshapen, trunk awry, branches streaming all in one direction like witch's hair. One thinks inevitably of an old actress, resplendent onstage, but after the performance, stripped of wig, makeup and costume, a crone like any other.

Geese! Geese! we cry, the first to spy them calling to alert the others. We look up into the infinite sky and see a skein, forming and reforming, in a continual undulation. The crescendo of trumpeting calls forth one of the primal responses in the human breast. It is an archaic warning, the alarm sounded by those fleeing before some dreadful calamity. We standing below, wingless, chilled by the knowledge of approaching ice and death, are pledged to stay, to do battle with the forces of the Arctic, but we cannot deny, for all our contemporary safety devices, a knot of instinctive fear in our guts.

The eerie music attenuates, the geese grow smaller and at last invisible against the shimmer of high air and cloud, the echo of their cries ringing in our ears as we still strain to follow their flight. The silence which comes then is filled with a kind of wonder and apprehension. We shake ourselves, smile ruefully, and go back to our tasks with renewed urgency, for winter is that much closer.

A fire has been going for three days in the dining room, heavy new logs placed on the embers of the old around the clock. In the kitchen, the wood range radiates its comfortable heat and keeps kettle and soup pot simmering. It is not winter yet, no snow or sub-zero temperatures, but one feels the raw chill more acutely in this transitional time, grateful for the shelter of warm interiors.

Rising at six, which was so lately five, the barns and outbuildings seem hulks stranded on a nacreous tide of moonlight, the skeletal trees blackened driftwood, the willows wracks of seaweed. The silence has a drowned quality. But the light changes, the moon swims into invisibility as a pale dawn takes possession of the sky, the rimed waves flatten into fields and vast dunes are once more revealed as hillsides.

The silence is shattered by Mr. MacGregor wildly announcing that Gallagher, having leaned greatly against the pasture fence, has spent this moonlit night in the orchard with the deer, gorging on windfalls. So the first task is to catch him. The second is to mend fence. Again.

Telephone.

"I'm up here at Falcon Ridge Colony and I'd like permission to hunt your place with bow and arrow."

"No. We don't allow bow-and-arrow hunting."

"You *don't?*" Momentary silence while the caller puzzles over such a curious response to what is surely to him the ultimate in sportsmanship. I do not elaborate, but my mind is spinning with pictures of deer, impaled by the shaft that did not quite kill, coursing the upper reaches of our hill, seeking shelter in the familiar forest, where a prolonged and agonizing death awaits.

"Well, how about the rifle season later?"

"No." I can barely get out a polite "Sorry."

"But your signs say 'Hunting by Permission Only...'"

"We let two or three neighbors we know well hunt here. That's all."

"Oh. Well. Okay..."

Click.

Every year we discuss this decision, the pros, the cons. We are acutely aware of all the arguments for keeping the deer population from outgrowing the carrying capacity of the land. We know that the deer have been growing smaller in the past few years, as competition for browse increases; roads, housing developments and ski resorts have taken over some of their habitat, and the interfaces between woodland and field which provide ideal feeding conditions are diminishing as forest reclaims farmland. And with the extermination of their natural predators, bears, wolves, bobcats, the only predator left to trim the herds is man himself. We know that a swift death by rifle in the fall is preferable to starvation in February. As for bow-hunting, one of our favorite local youths says, "I figure it gives the deer a better chance."

Yet to give permission for the shooting of a buck who has made our hill acres his kingdom, and who has somehow survived all the odds of nature to arrive at a nobly antlered maturity, seems a betrayal. There is nothing more alive than a buck, poised in an instant before flight, alert in every fiber of his being. And there is nothing deader than a buck, blind-eyed, stiff, trussed across the hood of a victorious hunter's vehicle.

Yet we know that many a local family counts on venison in the freezer to get through the winter. They have hunted these hills for over two hundred years. Who are we, with our bleeding hearts, to post this land they knew long before us?

So every year we compromise. We give permission to a handful of hunters who have always hunted here, whom we know to be expert and responsible. It is not an ideal solution. Perhaps there isn't one.

I like the kind of dinner party you can have around here, where the guests are qualified to converse on a range of topics from the nuclear weapons freeze campaign, with a digression on the national deficit, to a consideration of which are dumber, chickens or sheep, with a digression on the sagacity of pigs.

Two weeks ago the Silas Clark house caught fire in the middle of the night and was totally destroyed. We saw the smouldering remains next day. The barns, kennels and flagpole stood near, untouched, looking somehow blank and exposed with the disappearance of the house which had been the focus of the homestead. Today when we drove by, there was no sign of the ruins. The site had been bulldozed, filled in and graded. Except for the big square of topsoil bare in the middle of the surrounding grass, there was nothing to indicate that a capacious house once stood there sheltering generation after generation.

This prompt dealing with catastrophe, tidying up, going on to the next job, is characteristic of one kind of New Englander. Time is not wasted on mourning that for which there is no remedy. Too much calls for attention in other areas to dwell on tragedy; its evidences are cleared away so that scars will not evoke comment or commiseration. Survive and go on. That's the rule. It was what Dorothy Canfield Fisher meant when she said of Vermonters that "above all they are Anglo-Saxon in ruling out self-pity from among the permissable emotions."

We hear Silas has already arranged for a prefabricated ranch house to be erected where the old house stood. It won't be the same, but Mrs. Clark expects it will be a whole lot easier to keep up to her standards of cleanliness.

Brightness has drained out of the landscape. The last hurrah is sounded by the golden tamaracks here and there, startlingly loud in the muted surroundings. Once they have dropped their needles, the quietude will be complete.

Now the hills are great shabby animals, bears, yaks, bison, tranquilly stretching shoulders and flanks against the sky. Their heavy pelts are marked in patches and folds of cinnamon, sable, and a kind of violet-tinged brown that seems to belong only to this season. The vast beast-shapes at rest are a protective encirclement; one is almost persuaded of a silent, cosmic chewing of cud.

In the town hall the voting booths are put up and I as one of the poll-watchers help to check off the names of registered voters, those who have taken the Freeman's Oath of Vermont. There is quite a steady stream of them, some of whom I am embarrassed to have to ask about their names, and not just the newcomers either. The town clerk never has to do this. She has every one of the thousand citizens of this town filed in her memory, and sized up as well.

One of the poll-watcher's duties is to assist, in strictly non-partisan fashion, those who request help in voting by reason of failing eyesight, loss of pencil, or general confusion over the different colors of ballots for state, county and local offices. When in mid-morning Agatha Winthrop comes in — *comes* is too mild a word, for this octogenarian sails into the room like a full-rigged clipper ship — she announces that because of her tiresome cataracts she will need someone to read off the names of the candidates.

The two of us squeeze into a booth and I draw the skimpy black curtain. I do not get very far in my task before I sense a certain impatience on Agatha's part as I go through the list, which has a good sprinkling of candidates whose names reveal that their ancestors came from such places as Poland, France or Italy. Very soon, Agatha speaks out in a contralto that can be heard throughout this small corner of a democracy created by immigrants:

"Just give me the American names. There are too many foreigners in the government already."

Hank and Maud Warren came for a midday meal Saturday and it was good to see them enjoying a respite from chores. Hank hoped he'd be able to finish everything the menu included, especially the pumpkin pie, and have time for a little visiting before he had to get back to the barn for evening milking.

"Man has to be a little crazy to keep on farming in this climate, with these taxes and land prices, and help so hard to get," he declared, shaking his head.

"Where else would you rather be?" we asked. He thought it over, helping himself to more coffee. He named a few places — California, Florida. Texas maybe. But they were only names. He didn't really want to go to those alien acres. He knew himself at home here in Vermont, with all its rigors. He'd never "belong" anywhere else.

He is kin to the farmer described 130 years ago by Thoreau: "A man of New England probity and worth, immortal and natural like a natural product, like the sweetness of a nut, like the toughness of hickory...Moderate, natural, true, as if he were made of earth, stone, wood, snow."

And his hill farm may be, like Thoreau's neighbor's, "only fit to hold the world together." But "his lean soil has sharpened his wits." And besides, "you see heavens at a lesser angle from the hill than from the vale."

That must be what keeps some of the best from giving up, selling out, and moving on. But the average farmer, like Hank, is in his fifties. What about the upcoming generation?

I talked to a 17-year-old the other day who would dearly love to farm. But his family has sold off most of their property, and he knows he will never have enough money of his own to buy a viable farm. "It just isn't a living anymore anyway," he said, justifying his pessimism. "Besides," he added, "who'd ever want to marry me?"

George Washington said, "The life of the Husbandman, of all others, is the most delightful. It is honorable, it is amusing, and, with judicious management, it is profitable." Certainly it is honorable, infinitely more so than the careers to which so many lives are devoted today, which wittingly or not contribute only to a grossly consumerist society or to preparation for little wars or the ultimate one. As for profitable, you would have a hard time finding even the most judicious manager agreeing that farming produces returns commensurate with investment and labor.

But amusing? Yes, when you think about it, the life of the Husbandman generally is that if we take amuse to mean "hold the attention agreeably, stir with pleasing emotions, please, entertain, divert, beguile, interest, occupy, engross, absorb, cheer, charm, gladden, recreate, enliven, solace, gratify, exhilarate, rejoice, do one's heart good," as it is defined in one thesaurus. He may never think to put it in those terms, but surely some of these elements are truly there in the calling to which he is committed, or the Husbandman would never be able to stick out the intervals when it is not in the least diverting, solacing, or beguiling, even while it is engrossing, absorbing, and holding his attention.

The interest and the satisfactions do, for most farmers, outweigh the liabilities. It is a pity that only 3% of the population knows that. It was nearer 90% when George was alive.

In a factual declaration of what was, and still is, national policy, one Undersecretary of Agriculture set us all straight several years ago. With unusual candor, he said, "I think it is a mistake to go too far in trying to keep people on the farm when it doesn't make sense economically. We should just recognize the fact we are going to have fewer people making a living farming...We do not have any moral obligations to patches of land."

Fraudulent, surely, but nonetheless welcome, this trio of days disguised as summer. The sun is so warm and generous that one's bones relax involuntarily from the tension they have been practicing in preparation for north winds and blizzards. These days are an unforeseen gift, almost unmerited. We are going to be allowed a period of grace to do those things which we ought to have done ere now, those tasks of tidying up after summer and preparing for winter which, had we been properly organized, would by now have been complete.

We scramble about, cleaning up, shoring up, gathering in, winterizing barn, sheds and house. What a blessing, this Indian summer! In other years, by this date all might have been frozen hard, even snowed in with the first blizzard, and here we are moving about with the temperature nearly seventy. We can only savor each hour, and keep an eye on the western sky, which will surely announce a change shortly. But tonight's sunset is of disarming softness, hills and trees silhouetted against a tender peach translucence, a crescent moon hanging in the still-blue upper reaches. Winter is dawdling somewhere to the north and for the moment we forget that he always eventually keeps his engagements.

An enterprising young resident of our town has taken his tape recorder out into the night to capture the eerie sounds of coyotes. These emigres from the west are certainly audible, if seldom visible. We hear their unmistakable howls on clear nights, and once, when the moon was cold and full, we were awakened by what sounded like a throng of coyotes in full cry crossing below the pond into the woods, in pursuit, we thought, of deer. But the game warden, who says there are sixteen of them living in the hills and hollows encircling the town, tells us they live in pairs rather than packs and that there is no evidence that they have caused any damage whatsoever to deer or to livestock, since their diet consists principally of rabbits and small rodents.

Out in New Mexico, where coyotes are far more numerous, there is a group of men calling themselves the Artesia Varmint Hunters Association. They consider coyote hunting a sport, as well as a favor to sheep and cattle ranchers. These hunters have developed a special whistle that imitates the wailing squeal and squall of a wounded jackrabbit. It attracts the coyotes, who are then easily picked off with shotguns or high-powered rifles. The hunters feel they are performing a public service and would be proud if they exterminated the coyotes entirely. In other areas out west mass poisoning of coyotes and other predators has long been accepted practice.

In opposition to this kill-'em-off attitude, Dr. George Schaller of the New York Zoological Society defends coyotes as among the most useful of wildlife managers. He is keenly aware of the distaste for predators and a general misunderstanding of their role. "I have heard it argued," he says, "that education will change the feeling of the populace toward predators. But when I see the mass-poisoning of coyotes by the U.S. government in the western states, and the irrational harrying of the puma by cattle ranchers, I question the efficacy of that pronouncement." Dr. Schaller, who has listed many endangered species world-wide, feels a special urgency to learn as much as possible about vanishing fauna. "All too often in history," he observes, "the last of a species has disappeared into the belly of an ignorant hunter, its epitaph a belch. Perhaps our efforts to accumulate knowledge and rally in defense of endangered animals will ultimately result in a sound conservation program satisfactory to man and his livestock and also to wildlife. In either case, the efforts must be made now, for the same opportunities may well vanish in a decade."

Coyotes are probably too clever to be exterminated very soon, but they aren't all that safe in their new homes in Vermont. We hear vehement accusations against them by our friends who are in the sheepraising business. And every year now the Vermont newspapers with their photographs of triumphant Nimrods displaying their quarry — bucks and bears — include pictures of very dead coyotes, hanging upside down from the outstretched arms of hunters who cannot conceal their atavistic pride.

The trees in the woods stand in an anticipatory hush. After the green rush of spring and summer productivity, after the celebratory brilliance of the fall, comes an interim of relinquishment and fatigue. In the time that follows the trees take on a quality of stripped-down mutual readiness, almost an eagerness, for the oblivion of winter. Is it fanciful to think that they know what is coming? They seem so wise in their silence, standing in expectant ranks as far as the eye can see uphill and down dale, so true to themselves and loyal to one another, possessed of a knowledge so much more ancient than any known to us, so accepting of their duties and all weathers and seasons. Standing amongst them, that restive newcomer, the human being fraught with questions and distractions, finds in their calm assurance a certain comfort in the November dusk.

This morning early, a shot, sounding terrifyingly close. The echoes reverberate for a long time, then the explosion is followed by another and another in quick succession.

The pretty, mild weather continues. I long to go walking in the woods, but dare not. Already three hunters have died from gunshot accidents, and a number injured. A seventeen-year-old girl lies in hospital gravely wounded. She had been walking along the river with her mother. "I thought she was a deer," the hunter explains. And as always, elderly men with their rifles are found lifeless back in the woods — heart attacks. Cows, horses and dogs are not safe.

It is a deadly season altogether.

For a trinity of raindays, we saw the world in tones of grey, pelting, swirling, enfolding. To waken this morning to a world gone white was a shock. It is always a shock, that first snow, the clang of a great gate closing on life and growth. It snowed wetly all day, until by twilight there were six inches obliterating the outlines of roads, walls, pastures and fields.

In the post office, villagers yank off crusted mittens to unlock their mailboxes.

"How's the road up your way? Heard it was pretty bad over Brandon Gap."

"Snow's heavier than last year for a first. Hate to see it, but I guess we had to pay for that Indian summer."

"Hunters happy, I guess, with the tracking so easy."

"Got my wood in the shed, apples in the cellar, tarpaper on the north side, popcorn on the shelf. *I'm* ready for winter."

Sparkle everywhere as cloudless skies preside over the snow-mantled land and the sun sequins the still open waters of the pond. By noon the melt has bared expanses of green and eaves and branches drip in accelerated rhythm. Blocks of snow break off from the roof and slide to the ground in bumptious crashes. But the thermometer does not venture far into the forties, and by evening a freeze calls a halt to all that playful nonsense. Puddles congeal into glass, fondued surfaces of snow harden, and winter is in control once more.

As the afternoons grow shorter and chillier we gravitate earlier to the hearth and the consolations of tea. We generally make do with ordinary tea in mugs, but sometimes break out the Earl Grey or Lapsang Suchong in proper cups. Whatever, we agree with Sydney Smith, the English writer who waxed eloquent on the subject around the beginning of the nineteenth century: "Thank God for tea! What would the world do without tea? How did it exist? I am glad I was not born before tea!"

It is, except for water, the world's cheapest and most popular drink, whether made in a samovar, a Spode teapot, or a battered tin can over a bush fire. A Japanese master of the tea ceremony says of it that "tea has not the arrogance of wine, the self-consciousness of coffee, nor the simpering innocence of cocoa." Samuel Johnson said of himself that he was "a hardened and shameless tea-drinker...who with tea amused the evening, with tea solaced the midnight, and with tea welcomed the morning." Gladstone took to bed each night a hot-water bottle containing tea. When his feet were warm, he drank the contents.

So we feel we are in good company with such advocates. We know what the formidable philosopher Francis Bacon meant when he spoke of it so humanly: "Some comforting drink at four o'clock, which is the hour of my declining, were proper for me."

How capricious! Autumn has circled around for a reprise. Snow still on the heights, and northside of walls and barns, but the afternoon grows balmier instead of chillier, dissolving toward an opalescent sunset. Tonight the air is intoxicatingly soft, sounds carry like endearments across the valley, and a ringed moon invites one to stay out and dance under its ethereal light. Sarah Bernhardt could not have made a more dramatic comeback.

When I must be, for more than a few hours, in the city, I find myself constantly thinking about how things are affecting *me*. *I* am assaulted by the noise, *I* am defiled by the pervasive dirt, *I* am outraged by the contrasts between luxury and deprivation, by the alienated street population, by the fear and sheer man-made ugliness on every hand. *I* am constantly reacting violently to evidence of violence.

In the country, I am generally less conscious of myself. Reactions seem to take place on a different, deeper level. I am responding to stimuli and events that are natural, cyclical, cosmic, not threatening and agitating in a personal sense. What my vision encompasses is no longer of a limited human character, so the responses are less limited to merely human concerns. Feelings seem to be part of something much larger and infinitely more important, an interaction that is without an element of deliberate confrontation. It is the difference, I venture, between the fragmentation of life in the city and the wholeness that may be found in the natural world beyond it.

"Buy a piece of Vermont!" urge the real estate advertisements. "Buy land — they aren't making any more of it!" And, moved by their various needs, people do buy pieces of Vermont, just as we did.

We can't feel, now that we are here, that the door should be shut and nobody else allowed in. We are generally pleased when people find Vermont their spiritual home, purchase a house, plunge enthusiastically into what they think are native ways, then settle down and mellow, becoming part of the scenery like everyone else. We may find the massive seasonal influx of skiers a trial at times, and regret the transformation of some villages into hard-edged resort towns, but we know that many of the skiers truly love Vermont, returning to their city jobs refreshed and strengthened by the hills, and we know too how much the state's economy depends upon the presence of these temporary residents. "Second homes" may not always be a luxury to their owners, but necessary havens to productive people who need quiet intervals and closeness to the earth to continue their significant work elsewhere.

We are well aware of Vermont's unique attractions. We know they are not "ours," they are God-given and not to be denied to anyone from anywhere.

But what can be hard to accept is the view of Vermont (or Colorado or Arizona or anyplace endowed with natural splendors) as so much land to be grabbed up and exploited for profit. Land has always been bought and held as investment by prudent property-holders, and of course there was a lot of pretty questionable acquisition and profit-making in the early days — Ethan and Ira Allen were very successful at this sort of thing when the state was still largely wilderness, beckoning the post-Revolutionary wave of settlers. But land is scarcer, more precious nowadays, and we have many more fiendish ways of despoiling it. The need for protection is more vital than ever.

Most Vermonters place a high value on conserving the land, and there are environmental laws which have done much to prevent the worst excesses. But there are still "loopholes," still people willing to sell out, still entrepreneurs with out-of-scale visions which take no account of the character of this place.

Vigilance is required at all times. There is nothing sentimental or even impractical about the concept of the sanctity of the land. They really aren't making any more of it.

The untimely light in the room woke me after midnight, the windows squares of radiance. I rose and looked out into a miracle. "Come, look!" I cried. "Northern lights!" Sleep had no hold over this sort of spectacle. We thrust arms into bathrobes and raced downstairs with sashes flying.

Oh, how cold it was out there under the sky! But such a sky! Bright, bright as daylight, but of a refulgence never seen by day. And pulsating, throbbing, vast bands of celestial green light rippling, playing over the immensities of space. The stars shone brilliantly when they were not veiled by the waves of green.

How rapidly the colors shifted and swirled over half the vault of heaven! It was as if these immense ribbons of light were orchestrated to unheard music — adagio, agitato, andante. Almost you could hear the music — a universal harmony. And it was fraught with the possibilities of meaning. Some kind of apocalyptic message was being beamed to us from beyond the Arctic circle. It was too awesome and urgent to be a mere physical phenomenon, a simple eruption of gaseous flares.

Intensely exhilarated, we stood, dwarfed and vulnerable, straining to hear, willing to swear there was truly a titanic melodic humming. We watched in a kind of mesmerized state until at last frost crept into our bones and with a feeling that it was nearly blasphemous not to remain we did go back into the warmth of our bed.

The telephone rang. It was Harry, the city editor of the Rutland newspaper, whose workday is never over before midnight. Driving homeward, he had stopped to call and tell us of the northern lights he was seeing.

"Yes, thank you, yes, we saw them! Have they ever been more fantastic?"

This was front-page news!

Thanksgiving is a five-day affair here, with friends and kin beginning to arrive Wednesday and mostly staying through Sunday. In addition to whatever family turns up, there are several particularly cherished friends who traditionally celebrate this holiday with us, sometimes the only time each year that we see them. This concentrated period gives rise to a congenial intimacy that we all find very precious.

Everyone helps. There is the turkey to be stuffed with dressing flavored from the garden herbs hanging in stiff bunches from the kitchen beams — sage, marjoram, summer savory, parsley. There are squashes to be hacked up, onions to be peeled, potatoes to be prepared, cranberries to be simmered, apples to be polished. When two tables have been put together down the length of the dining room, the extra-long white damask cloth is brought out for its annual appearance, and one or two people with a knack for artistic arrangement are put to work constructing a bountiful centerpiece of all the fruits of the season. The crystal and silver sparkle, fires on all the hearths crackle, and the house is filled with the fragrances of the kitchen mingled with that of the chrysanthemums in every room.

When on Thursday evening we at last gather at the candlelit table it is a moment of high joy. Sometimes we sing our grace — *Praise God from whom all blessings flow* — fortissimo. Sometimes William says a thoughtful grace which always includes an invocation of peace. Sometimes it is his brother Christopher, a Catholic priest, who has his own affecting eloquence. One year everyone found a slip of paper and a pencil at his place and was asked to write down what he was most thankful for at this moment. While they dined, people were thinking about this and taking a moment to put down their responses. Then the notes were gathered and over the pumpkin pie William read them out, anonymously.

It was a moving experience. The causes for gratitude were varied: For health. For a recent cease-fire in the Middle East. For the opportunity to grow. For my grandparents. For my children. For the distilleries of Scotland. For my lover. For becoming an uncle. For the devotion of my wife. For water and sunshine. For turkeys — and doves. For work I love. For the miracle of love between two people, within a family, for friends, and for all mankind. For those who reach for peace. For Vermont. For being alive and in the best possible surroundings today.

For the following days we move in a heightened atmosphere of sharing. There are hours of wood-chopping, hill-climbing, resting, eating. And talking, talking. At all hours there will be long, eager conversations going on in kitchen, dining room, living room, bedroom, and the open air. And one night will be devoted to our annual histrionics — the Barton Hill brand of charades, complete with makeshift costumes and props and fierce competition between teams to present the most dramatic and insoluble performances. Since everyone participating is imaginative, intelligent and endowed with a sense of the comic, these dramas reach such a high point of hilarity we all quite often collapse in helpless heaps with laughter.

Then, as in the Farewell Symphony, people begin to pack up and leave, the good-byes prolonged, and sometimes postponed for a day or two should we have inclement weather. When they have all left, the house subsides into what seems an unnatural quiet for a time, but filled with a great warmth that lingers, sometimes until the next Thanksgiving.

Winter

With chain saw down by the pond, we cut up branches of elm strewn in the snow, the big segments from the trunk having already been transported to the woodshed. These more slender limbs are marked for stove lengths, and a plenty of them there is to be had for the cutting. Elm of course hasn't a favorable reputation as firewood, but Vermont cordwood expert David Tresemer says that "the fuel value of one pound of oven-dried wood is the same for all species, about 8600 BTUs...Unless firewood is bought by volume, in which case species means a great deal, the best course is to burn what is available." What is available here in greatest quantity is elm, and so we utilize it, often mixing it with maple or other hardwoods, and, with William's constant and experienced attention, it has kept us warm for years.

We work cheerfully through the relatively mild afternoon, William quick and deft with his noisy machine, I picking up each foot-long rough-barked log to pile in the back of the Bronco. When we have a respectable load, William proposes we stop and drive homeward (it is nearing teatime), but I point out there is quite a pile of potential stovewood still remaining. So we continue working, cutting up the skinnier branches and broken remnants.

All the time I am thinking of the women we used to see in North Africa, trotting along the rudimentary roads, bent nearly double under immense brushy heaps of faggots they had gathered somewhere back in the barren countryside or far up on the sparsely wooded hills. These women, with their long vividly colored skirts and proud Berber faces, often started out at daybreak, travelling miles and spending the entire day pursuing the least little twig, for this was the only fuel they had to cook their tajine and couscous. They were contemporaries in a 2000-year line of foragers. Their predecessors had been, along with the goats, denuding the valleys and mountains since the Phoenicians first came to those shores. The advance troops of the Roman conquerors reported that this land was entirely green and forested, but it did not take many generations of soldiers and settlers to fell so many trees for fires and construction that the valleys were stripped to desert and the bones of the Atlas Mountains exposed to the relentless sun. Now there are government-sponsored efforts at reforestation, and with the discovery of oil and gas beneath the sand, finding fuel may not be much longer the desperate task it has been for so many overburdened women for centuries. Yet I would guess that North Africans may never come to regard wood carelessly again; I hope they will not.

Here we are, in the middle of Vermont, surrounded by millions upon millions of trees, apparently an inexhaustible supply for our stoves, furnaces, even our factories and power plants, and yet I do not take one single tree lightly. Each one is a miracle, as an essential part of the cycle of rain and air and water, as protection against erosion, as builder of soil, source of multiple uses to man, shelter for birds and beasts, and an essential element in the dear beauty of this landscape. From this dead elm we are salvaging I do not wish to waste one sprig big enough for burning, and so we keep on adding to our store until the back of the Bronco can hold no more.

Then it is back to tea by the fireside, where the wood gives us the oldest heat man knows how to make. I remember the words of a Cabot farmer: "I like the feel of wood heat, for one thing, because it's a different heat. It penetrates you, and makes you warm. It *gives* you the heat." It is true that you get an immediate, tangible interaction with the source, which is not the same sort of thing you have with diffused central heat. Besides, as old Homer said in something like the 7th century B.C., "A blazing fire makes a house look more comely upon a winter's day, when the son of Cronos sends down snow."

Keys — old keys — boxes of forlorn leftovers, kept because — because the moment might come when a key from this ill-assorted collection might prove to be the very one, the only one, to open a box, a drawer, a door, that will give us what has been long lost or mislaid in our lives, give us treasures, give us answers. We are afraid to throw away these rusting, enigmatic bits of metal, for if we do, the next day we will find a keyhole of need or promise, and the only key to open it will have disappeared forever, with no one to blame but ourselves.

Abed for three days with the 'flu' that is "going around," I think of the early settlers felled, as they often recorded in letters and memoirs, by the bone-breaking chills and fevers of what they called ague. Isolated, far from physicians, they had of course their home remedies, and many did survive this debilitating disease. But in the face of other, more serious illnesses, they were often helpless. What happened when a father with diabetes could no longer plant and hunt? When a mother with cancer of the breast was too ill to care for her children? When someone died in midwinter and the frozen earth and high drifts made burial impossible? There are tales of these sufferings in all the old documents, and they make a modern reader shudder, marveling at the toughness which enabled these hardy folks to carry on.

In a way which is difficult for us to imagine, our ancestors lived in the constant presence of death, with little defense against disease and injury, infant mortality, plagues and epidemics, war and famine. But this was death of individuals, sometimes brutally multiplied, but fathomable. Except for Millerites and such, they did not have an expectation of the end of the world, or mass extermination, which might come at any moment. Increasingly since Hiroshima, we have lived with such an expectation, and it becomes daily more probable as our leaders insanely pile up nuclear armaments and grow ever more careless in their thinking and in their threats. All the grand immunities we have acquired from diphtheria, malaria, tuberculosis, typhoid fever and the rest of the old killers avails us little now when there is no vaccination, no miracle drug, against nuclear holocaust. We take our children to pediatricians to insure their health, we save the lives of heart and kidney patients with complex operations and organ transplants, we prolong the years of the elderly with magical medications. Yet for one great illness, human folly, we seem to have no cure, and we may all be charred and irradiated within the hour because of it.

A week of impossibly fickle weather, beginning with a balmy April day in which the earth heaved and gave back the frost it had gathered. Roads running with melt, ruts deepening hazardously, the barnyard a chocolate swamp. Then sweet vernal rains misting the air, gentle enough to allow working outdoors. Next day, torrents of rain, lashing winds, rising waters. A Wednesday morning of plummeting temperatures, the air filled with infinitesimal needles of ice. Flurries of snow, gusts of wind. Thursday the thermometer at ten below, a thin, mean curtaining of snow, and bone-snapping wind. The cold holding all night under a glittering moon, the temperature dropping to eighteen below with a frightening wind chill factor. I honestly thought, coming back from the barn that barely sheltered the horses from the wind knifing in at every crack, that my fingers had been frostbitten in a matter of minutes. All day a cold so piercing any activity outdoors was a matter of grim endurance, and indoors a pervasive chill in all the corners no matter how the fires were stoked.

Feeling truly in winter's grip, I knew a profound sympathy across the centuries with the nameless poet who wrote around the year 1300 a lament for the season. I found it in a collection of English poetry, and it begins:

Wynter wakeneth al my care;
Nou thise leves waxeth bare;
Ofte I sike and mourne sare
When hit cometh in my thoht
Of this worldes joie, hou hit geth al to noht.

I labored over deciphering it from the ancient language, and managed something of a translation:

Winter wakens all my care,
Now these trees all stand so bare.
Oft I sit in sore despair
When comes to my thought
Of this world's joy, how it goes all for nought.

Now it is, and now it is not,
As if it had never been begot;
How many that say, Thus man's lot:
All goes by God's will;
All must die, though we like it ill.

All my grain that grew so green,
How soon is gone, the field left clean;
Jesu, help that it be foreseen,
And shield us from hell!
For I know not whither I must go, nor how long here I dwell.

Not a time of good cheer for anybody or anything. Even the blue jays are subdued, flying low and too cold to scream.

Driving along Vermont highways, sometimes between great rock faces that have been cleft by road engineers, one sees the geological foundations upon which we live and have our being — awesome in their ossified embodiment of glacial violence and unimaginable eons of entirely inhuman events, yet also deeply comforting in their revelation of what solid strength we have built upon.

In a very direct way we come upon fragments of the prehistoric past when we plough our fields and dig in our gardens. No matter how successfully we have cleared the ground the year before, each spring we find new stones that have worked their way to the surface. "Best crop we grow, stuns," the New England farmer grumbles. It makes one ache to look at the walls built from the rocks and boulders pried from the soil of these hill farms. Thousands upon thousands of stones, each one in the wall representing a problem and a solution.

On our place there are not only walls but great middens of stone, heaped in odd corners, awaiting God knows what use. They tend to mingle with time into an almost indistinguishable heap, lichen blanketing the exposed surfaces, briars springing up around them, an occasional sapling finding enough nourishment to push its way up and stand, scrawny but triumphant, atop the tumulus. Elsewhere there are immense boulders left in place where they grew in the fields, having defied pre-mechanized efforts to dislodge them.

In the woods and uplands there are many more of these enormous hulks, some appealingly sculptured by time and weather, often adorned by mosaics of moss and lichen. There they repose, emanating a kind of permanent dignity that commands respect. Why? A rock is only a collection of inanimate minerals. Or is it? I can quite imagine all its infinitesimal particles being capable of vibrating, humming in primordial life.

Once Spinoza asked, "Can a stone think?" Perhaps not. But if it can, if it does, surely its thoughts are not only ancient but wise.

"The North Wind shall blow, and we shall have snow, And what will poor robin do then, poor thing?" And what shall the rest of us do, who can't hide our heads under our wings?

The Greeks were grateful to Boreas, the god who personified the North Wind, putting on festivals in his honor, because he swept away enemy fleets. It is a little difficult to imagine Vermonters sponsoring such a festival. Elizabethan poet Edmund Spenser in his "Shepherd's Calendar" describes how "blustering Boreas doth encroche" upon the pastoral landscape, and we know all about that encroachment.

Atop Mount Horrid, snow is blasted across rock outcroppings, and throughout the valley the wind finds long tunnels to swoop through like a thundering, whistling express train. Limbs crash from skeletal elms, moss grows thick upon the exposed flanks of sugar maples, saplings are contorted into anguished shapes. The deer huddle under the spruce boughs, and grow lean.

Every hillside becomes a Wuthering Heights, Emily Bronte explains the title of her novel thus: "Wuthering Heights is the name of Mr. Heathcliff's dwelling, 'wuthering' being a significant provincial adjective descriptive of the atmospheric tumult to which its station is exposed in stormy weather." The word "whither" or "whuther" was brought into the English language by early Scandinavian invaders, and as a noun it means a violent or impetuous movement, a rush, attack, onset, smart blow or stroke, a blast, a gust of wind, a quivering or trembling, a rushing or whizzing sound." All of these and more we sometimes experience simultaneously on Barton Hill.

We lie abed, kept sleepless by the rattling window panes, the creaking beams, the shivering of the frame from ridge to foundation, and those sudden ferocious attacks of supreme velocity which will surely rip off the roof. By day a trip to the barn is a battle of wills, and the children, bundled up and sent out to play, are soon back at the door, icy tears streaming down their reddened cheeks.

So here we are, really only on the threshold of winter, already chilled to the bone. But there are those who will not be daunted. We are heartened by the sight of Marjorie Lynott, well into her seventies, setting off on her cross-country skis, shouting above the wind: "Florida? You couldn't pay me to go there! This is the place for all seasons!"

To be greeted on a December morning by a broadcast of Mozartean melody interpreted by the pipes of Pan — well, that is enough to set an exhilarating tone for the day. To hear those joyous, soaring notes played by a contemporary musician on an instrument of such antiquity dramatizes the timeless nature of music and the magic ability of technology to embody and disseminate it.

The pipe is the closest extension of the human voice, dependent on the breath of life to create its sound. The player must literally breathe every note, a very different act from drawing music from bow and string or drumhead. The whistle that can be fashioned from a blade of grass was surely even earlier. Its sound I remember from long ago. Sitting beside a green stream, my father cupped his hands before his lips in a gesture that even by a child could be recognized as atavistic, as a shrill squealing from the strand of grass pierced the summer air. On another day, he cut reeds, showing us how to section them into lengths of seven inches or so, and to make a notch at a precise height in the narrow cylinder. From this came sounds capable of some modulation even by children more eager than musical, and our primitive notes echoed merrily over the water.

When I lived in the Andes, I heard musicians produce haunting sounds from instruments new to me — tiples, tambours and pipes. These pipes were of bamboo, a graduated set of tubes bound together in the exact shape of the pipes blown by a cavorting Pan for dancing figures on a Grecian vase. With their massive chests and extraordinary control of breath, the Indians could extract from these pipes effortless melody of a long soulfulness. When I tried to blow on them, only a piteous sighing was evoked. There is still a set of these Colombian pipes here in our Vermont house, and from time to time someone attempts to play them, but the music is not there for casual musicians.

The *Oxford Companion to Music* says there is no wind instrument more ancient and none more widespread than the pan pipes; one source has them originating in China. Shepherds must have invented this beautifully shaped instrument, improving their skills in the long hours of watching over their flocks. Sheep cannot have been the most appreciative of audiences, and the shepherds must have rejoiced whenever they played for dancers on days of festival.

Pan, the god of shepherds, as the Greeks told the legend, pursued the Arcadian nymph Syrinx, but just as he thought to clasp her to his hairy bosom she cried out to her father, the river god Ladon, who transformed her into a reed. Pan, hearing the wind blow musically upon the reeds, cut them down and made them into pipes. Such pipes still bear the name of Syrinx, and we know it too as it comes down to us in the name of the family of plants with tube-like stems, lilac and syringa, which can still be cut into pipes and played by anyone inspired by Pan, or by Mozart.

As I stand at the kitchen sink and look out to the range of hills making a line which has been permanently imprinted upon my spirit, I think of the words of that hymn of Isaac Watts: *Before the hills in order stood/Or earth received her frame,/From everlasting Thou art God,/To endless years the same.*

These Green Mountains, the oldest in New England, first appeared about 440 million years ago and are geologically described as "truncated remnants of long north-south running folds in the bedrock crust." They have stood in order all those eons, but time has worn them down to lower heights and less craggy shapes than the younger White Mountains to the east or the Adirondacks to the west. Indeed the contours of these hills have been smoothed into conformations that are decidedly feminine. Almost any "typical Vermont landscape" will undulate: curving thighs, breasts at once seductive and maternal, a silhouette of a woman sleeping on her side — all these are constantly suggested, if not overtly, then by implication. It may explain why so many people arriving for the first time so immediately declare themselves "at home" here.

But however pleasing their shapes, these hills and mountains are not soft. They have sustained generations of farmers and woodsmen, but only at a price of persistent labor, defiant courage. The reward is sufficiency, little more, and the opportunity of finding, if one is not too busy surviving, an indigenous beauty wherever one looks. Within those voluptuous folds, atop those rounded peaks, many a life has been claimed, where human beings have climbed too high, ventured too far into the forest, stayed too long, flown too low. For all their enchanting forms, the hills have no need of us, and have every chance of outlasting us all.

Beyond the snow-covered hayfields, the mature pines and spruces stand singly or in groups up and down the hillside. A most handsome component of the white landscape throughout the winter, they shelter a host of seldom-seen wildlife. When I walk among them, I sometimes lift the low-sweeping boughs and peer into these places of refuge. The snow is patterned by a diversity of tracks leading in and out — skunks, squirrels, rabbits, blue jays, mice, and especially the deer. There is a quiet in these protected places, shadowed but with a lavender-tinged light reflected from the snow packed down by the resting bodies of the deer, strewn with bits of bark and needles, imprinted by small busy feet. I sometimes sense the presence of these wildings, observing me at a distance, perhaps having been disturbed only a moment ago. I do not stay long examining their hiding places. Sanctuaries should remain inviolate.

Stopping at Jake Dobson's little grey house right by the road to pick up some of his famous cider, I was invited to come in out of the cold while he searched in his kitchen for change. What a kitchen!

Dobson, long a widower, clearly does not wash his dishes until he runs out of plates, nor does he put away any food that might just as well be left on the table. The windows were caked with dirt, the curtains bedraggled, there were empty bottles on all the sills, and a heap of yellowing newspapers cascaded from a dangerously sagging ironing board.

But these domestic disarrangements were as nothing to the main feature of the room, which was an unbelievable collection of board-stiff coonskins stacked ten or twelve deep on chairs, bench, and floor, and extending into the parlor in one direction and the woodshed in the other. There were beaver and deerskins as well, but chiefly raccoons, their pelts stretched absolutely flat, their legs with the prehensile paws rigidly outthrust, their heads with the roguish masks slightly upraised, their bushy striped tails the finest things about them. There was a strong wild smell in the place which overcame any other odors that might have been expected as a result of the general disarray and neglect.

I had seen Jake's roadside sign — FURS BOT, BEST PRICES PAYED — but had never happened upon his business operations before. I was so taken aback at all this gross evidence that I did not at first notice that there was another old man in the kitchen, sitting on a stool next to the wood range sorting apples into a carton with hands that looked decidedly dirty and, yes, blood-stained. He like Jake was grizzled and small, wearing one checked flannel shirt atop another, the standard beaked cap on his head.

"Jake's got himself a good lot of skins, ain't he?" the oldster offered with a gap-toothed grin.

I collected myself and agreed that there were, indeed, a great many. "What do you do with them?" I asked Jake.

"Send 'em to Maine," Jake replied, rummaging in a paper bag which evidently served as a cash box.

"To Maine?"

"Yup. Big market for skins up there. They take all I can get. Matter of fact, Verne and me are goin' to take us a truckload over that way tomorra, if it don't snow."

"Thesen prime pelts," Verne told me. "Best kind of northern coon." Then he paused to wipe his nose on his sleeve and gave a cackle. "But I sure would like to git me some of them *southern* coons."

I couldn't believe my ears. Was this a Vermont redneck? There seemed to be an obvious racial implication here which was not the sort of thing one hears often in these parts, if at all.

I took my two quarters from Jake, noticing that his hands too were unmistakably unwashed and bloody, picked up my jug of cider and bade the two old fellows a rather hasty farewell.

All the way home I puzzled over this encounter. One of the good things about living here has been the absence of the kind of bigotry one can run into elsewhere at all levels. Vermonters are a generally tolerant people, viewing disparaties and eccentricities with less prejudice than most. They may not approve of some things, but they seldom gang up on individuals or groups solely on the basis of differences in religion, behavior, or color. The Vermont Constitution of 1777 forbade slavery 87 years before the Emancipation Proclamation. Vermont sent more soldiers, relative to its population, to the Union Army than any other state. Vermonters have for decades opened their homes to black children who come from the city to spend the summer in our villages and on our farms.

The fact remains that our black population is almost negligible (a black Vermonter is a rarity) and we have in no degree experienced the tensions over integration of Boston, New York, Detroit, Chicago.

Where could that old codger Verne have picked up his bigotry? I could not come up with any explanation until I was almost home. Then I realized that it must have been, could have been, the baleful effect of indiscriminate television viewing — all those news stories of riots and looting, flashed on screen with no adequate interpretation of the causes, those errors and crimes of history that explode into racial confrontations. I felt grieved by this thought, but also helpless to change it. I could only be thankful that Verne's kind of unthinking comment is so mercifully rare in what we like to think is the free air of these hills.

I am not sure I will serve that cider to the family.

Going out the front door this evening on the way to a meeting at the high school, we checked the thermometer as usual: six degrees. Inching down the icy hill, I had a moment of recognition that I was no longer mentally fussing about the cold, the winter driving conditions. The transitional period was over, I had entirely accepted the fact that it was winter.

I believe it was a set of Swedish statistics that proved that northerners are more likely to be mentally alert as a result of having to adjust to changes in temperature and humidity. If that is the case, Vermonters' brains should rank among the world's most agile.

At the village store: "Do you think it's going to snow?"

Nellie behind the counter, gravely doling out change for the newspaper: "I find it's better not to think."

At exactly three-thirty the western hills turn black, a crimson sun slides out of sight, the world is instantly dark and lonely in a glacial twilight.

Saturday's sagging grey blankets of clouds at last release their burden, a quiet, slow falling of snow, certainly not a blizzard, but piling up seriously. On Sunday morning, ten inches at least of perfect powder, a pre-Christmas gift that has the ski resorts in ecstacies.

Walking in the snowy wood in utter silence, the temperature minus seven. Suddenly the sound of tiny nails being hammered into a tiny coffin — a downy woodpecker at work on a silver birch.

After tea, a wide glowing sunset in the same colors that flame in the hearth. From its post by our gateway, the cottonwood's black tracery of limbs and twigs arches above the line of Brandon Gap, where the sky is most fiery. The colors seem to enjoy their own performance and stay for a long time, very gradually fading to ash.

We sit over the Sunday crossword puzzle, look up and discover snow beginning to fall in the dark outside the window. We put another log on the fire, smile at the thought of all the stove wood newly stacked by the kitchen door, and write in 27 down — *substance or satisfaction:* CONTENT.

In Boston, where we went to meet Molly and Skip and the boys at the airport and to do a bit of Christmas shopping, there was brilliant sunshine, fresh wind, streets and shops crowded with cheerful people, pleasant sales clerks, Salvation Army trumpets blaring, color and muchness everywhere — the city at its best. In one department store I overheard a woman saying to her companion, "I'm glad to be back in my old haunting grounds."

Ah, what a haunting ground Boston is! — filled with the ghosts of Samuel Sewall and Mary Dyer, Samuel Adams and Harrison Gray Otis, Henry Wadsworth Longfellow and Julia Ward Howe, Wendell Phillips and Theodore Parker, Henry James and Mrs. Jack Gardner, not to mention Honeyfitz Kennedy and Mayor Curley.

One has a palpable sense sometimes of their hovering overhead, surveying the enormous changes that have taken place, the impulses to growth that transformed the tiny community of brave and bigoted Puritans, planting themselves on the rocks between ocean and forest, into the sprawling, polyglot, vital metropolis it has become. If only these specters could materialize, just long enough for us to see them as they were, to apprehend their power and intellectual energy, to hear their voices in their own accents and timbres, telling us exactly what they think of the Boston of today, so different from the city they would have known at the stages of their own citizenship, and yet what it is because of what they, in their times, put into it.

The Quaker weekly which comes to us from London by airmail, its tissue-thin pages filled with writing of a very high order by British Friends, contains a section recording births, marriages and deaths which we always scan not simply for occasional news of friends but for its manner of expression which is very British and often very graceful. In the most recent issue I found this death notice:

TYSON. — December 10. Suddenly in his garden, Charles Tyson of Westington Old Manor, Chipping Campden, Gloucestershire. A meeting of thanksgiving for his life will be held at Broad Campden Meeting House on January 29 at 3 pm.

What a splendid way to depart this life — "suddenly in his garden"! We did not know Charles Tyson, but I picture him in the still mild weather of a Gloucestershire December, elderly (Quakers generally live to a great old age), kneeling beside the rosebushes he has lovingly tended for thirty years, making sure they are protected against the winter to come. Then *suddenly* he is seized by a shock of brightness, a great opening of light, into which his spirit rises and is embraced even while his hand lets drop the pruning shears and his body falls to the welcoming earth.

I cannot imagine a more desirable way of leaving this world — after a life of usefulness, in the act of caring for a tiny portion of creation — suddenly, in one's garden. To be followed, not by mourning of friends and family, but by a meeting of thanksgiving for one's life.

There is a healthy lack of vanity in what we know as "real Vermonters." Only if they are professionals and office workers, and then only during office hours, do the men wear business suits. Most males are comfortably, practically, and permanently attired in jeans, corduroys, and heavyweight work pants, flannel shirts, serviceable jackets and caps, which never seem to be new but long molded to the wearer's shape and nature. A knot of men at a coffee counter or an ox-drawing contest may look indistinguishable to a stranger's eye, but each man is very well known to the others, and assessed not for his tailoring but for his character.

As for the wives, none is thought the less of because she wears a skew-skirted cotton dress and old white socks and weighs 200 pounds. She is known and valued for what she is and does, her sure hand with a newborn calf, the lightness of her biscuits, the confidence of her children, her tireless pitching of bales during haying season, her reliability as treasurer of the church, her husband's trust.

Christmas preparations are carried on almost from the Monday after Thanksgiving to late Christmas Eve. There is plum pudding to make and store in a crock to mellow in brandy, Christmas coffee cakes in braided rounds stuffed with citron and currants, and a mountain of cookies — anise-flavored springerle with its quaint raised figures, Scottish shortbread, brownies enriched with pineapple and chocolate frosting, pecan rolls, tarts filled with mincemeat and cranberries, frosted ginger cookies in shapes of stars, fir trees, reindeer. There are Christmas cards to make — each year William draws a telling little sketch with a message of peace to go out to two hundred or so.

And gifts to wrap — so many of those, for we are 32 in the immediate family, not counting nieces, nephews, cousins, dear friends or neighbors. The smallest bedroom is taken over for wrapping and packing for mailing, and is soon a hopeless confusion of bright papers, presents, tags and lists. The presents are very often books, or products of the kitchen and garden, or warm mittens or sweaters, and sometimes sleds or skates, or, once, a long toboggan that will carry five or six screaming down the hill.

Then there is the matter of the Christmas tree, which involves an expedition to the woods to find the perfect specimen, ten or more feet tall, to be brought in and erected in the dining room under the lofty beamed ceiling. The tall stepladder is put in place for the stringing of lights, the ornaments brought up from their basement estivation, taken from boxes and tissues to be greeted once again and hung in place with much consultation and criticism on the part of all family members participating in this rite of making this year's tree the most resplendent ever.

There are trips to deliver gifts in the neighborhood, and visits from friends dropping in to leave their offerings of jam or pickles or syrup, and the daily haul from the post office bringing stacks of cards and mysterious packages. There is a carol service in the village church, its white interior lit by candles, a tall spruce tree decked with golden balls next to the organ. There are arrivals from afar, and reunions that restore the heart.

It is a grand time, a blessed time, but also a fatiguing time, with always too much trying to be done in too short a season. I was frankly weary one evening just before Christmas when I sat on the living room floor putting together a very large wreath of pine, spruce and juniper with trimming of cones, barberries, and small carved wooden birds, to be hung over the fireplace. It was a demanding task and everyone else seemed too busy to help.

But then Roger and Stuart came in and opened the old mahogany music box. With their fair heads bent they looked through the pile of big brass disks which provided the mechanical music great-grandparents had listened to, and took out those meant for Christmas. Carefully the boys placed them one by one under the metal arm that moved over the perforations to call forth the tunes, and they cranked the handle carefully.

Now the room was filled with the silvery sound of Hark the Herald Angels Sing, The First Nowell, and Silent Night. It was enchanting, as different from all the richly orchestrated carols we had heard broadcast all season as a small chorus of very young cherubs would be from a full choir of harp-strumming angels.

I sat back and simply listened, letting the peaceful moments flow over and into my knotted spine, my buzzing brain, my fractured spirit. A remnant of that peace somehow remained with me through the rest of the holidays, giving them a beautitude that otherwise might have been missed.

Could it be that elders are no longer revered because there are so many of them? In the past, survivors to a great old age were far fewer and doubtless physically and mentally superior to those they'd outlived, as well as luckier. They really did have something of value to pass on to younger generations — how to escape from a saber-toothed tiger, which plants would cause healing or death, how to construct a shelter, what words to chant to appease the gods.

At La-Chapelle-aux-Saints a few years ago diggers found the skeleton of a Neanderthal man. Long past his prime, he was so bent over by arthritis that he could not possibly have taken part in the hunt. He had lost all but two of his teeth and could not have eaten without difficulty. But he had not been abandoned by his tribe. Anthropologists concluded that his companions provided food and "probably even softened it for him by partially chewing it." And there were traces of flowers which had been strewn in the grave, further evidence of the esteem and affection in which this elder of the tribe had been held.

Nowadays just about any fool can reach 70 or 80, and there are so many old people trying to be young rather than wise that the rest of the population can hardly be blamed for regarding them with something less than respect. And in any case, we no longer have to consult our elders when there are so many other ways to gain vital information from books, schools and universities, television, and thousands of experts all too eager to tell us how to eat, think, make love, bring up our children, and exterminate our enemies. In an age of computers, satellites, nuclear missiles and star wars, what have those whose peak of knowledgeability was reached even twenty years ago to tell a new generation about living in the present or preparing for the future? Old people as repositories of racial wisdom hardly exist any longer.

Or do they? Every now and again we hear a voice, read some words, that penetrate the electronic screen with which we have separated ourselves from the natural world and the old verities. We catch a phrase, an inflection, which comes through undistorted by technology, finding its way into that secret portion of our hearts that remains responsive to elemental claims. We recognize it as not out of date but timeless. Out of eight or nine decades of experience, some elder speaks with wisdom, reminding us of such concepts as duty, reverence, stewardship, compassion for the helpless, loyalty to family and to the human race, and we recognize their validity. It has nothing to do with politics, and everything to do with policy, and those of us struggling to administer a world of perilous complexities would do well to listen.

The new year has brought up nearly all the 39 varieties of snow for which the Eskimos have words. Early, a fall of heavy, wet snow was followed by enough melting to create a crust perhaps two inches thick. Walking became a kind of trail breaking, one footstep after another crushing through the resistant surface, leaving deep blue-tinted wells in the whiteness. Shins winced at the harsh scraping of jagged crust.

Down from the northeast slope of the hill the deer had made their way, those fragile-seeming legs and delicate hooves packing down a track a foot wide and nearly two feet deep. In the orchard, several trees have been circled, the snow churned and trampled as the deer nibbled bark and dug down to the layer of rotted apples beneath the white cover. They had rested here, too, their recumbent bodies carving out hollows, a strange poignance in those empty shapes. There were few other signs of life — a strand of chipmunk tracks leading out from a snow-rimmed hole along the stone wall, and quickly back again, and some old rabbit footprints.

The air was keen, the sky a blue which became ambivalent if one looked westward. A hint of more snow developed into reality the next day, this time in powder form. Once it cleared, walking became even more challenging. Putting down a foot meant going through some ten inches of fluff, to strike the stubborn crust below, then to drive into the densely packed wet substrata. Each step became an exercise in extrication, soon very tiring. Mr. MacGregor could make his way like a tugboat through the topmost powder, spraying white waves as he went, and seldom sinking through. This proved a help, and I struggled on behind in the trough he had fashioned.

We did not go far into the downhill pasture, but could see the horses had been able to plunge through to the open stream which bubbled icy black in little pools surrounded by still whiteness.

Yesterday, minus 16 in the morning, and later, a new snowfall, quite a different sort, with enormous flakes which, wherever they caught the light, glittered crystal and diamond. They came on for hours, and now the contours of the world became ever less evident under its persistent cover-up.

We drove unplowed and deserted roads to the Morgan's house which stood like a great lighted ocean liner locked in ice floes. The fireside talk and wine were warming, but we could see, beyond the windowpanes, the intransigent piling up of snow. Reading aloud from the town history the passage about David Barton freezing to death going home from the tavern in his sleigh in 1807 encouraged us to take an early departure.

The Bronco bucked along through the drifts, the headlights often dimmed by huge waves of snow rising furiously above the hood. All the windows were solid with lacings of frost. Christopher tried desperately to keep the windshield cleared by reaching out the window and working with his mittens. William gripped the wheel, straining to see the road in the flickering pathway of headlights piercing a tiny fraction of immense whirling whiteness in an immense blackness.

Landmarks obliterated, roadbed invisible, we slid and swerved and bulldozed our way down the mountain road, very glad indeed to reach the lighted streets of the snow-quiet village. Then it was out to the bridge and across the river and up our own hill with breath held and Bronco creaking and shaking. Home at last, our lane filled up with snow and the path to the doorway needing to be shoveled before we could get in. In the warm kitchen, we shared a posset before settling into beds.

This morning, still snowing. The fire in the kitchen stove ebbed out during the early hours, the chimney had gone cold and a great cap of snow built up over the opening, so thick that it closed off the flue entirely. Smoke from a fire started at breakfast time backed up into the kitchen; it was impossible to get up enough heat to melt through that white toque the chimney wears so jauntily. If it does not warm up during the morning, William will have to climb up with his ice rake and clear it off. Somehow the wires have not sagged and given way under this burden of snow, and we still have electricity, and coffee from a plugged-in percolator.

There have never been such depths overwhelming fields and woods and buildings. The maple trees clothed in white wool stand in a kind of daze, snow up to their knees. An abandoned robin's nest in a lilac bush supports a foot-high crown of white. We can scarcely see over the drifts to make out the curve of the pond below the house, and the spruces beyond it are wigwams of snow. The mountains are somewhere behind a curtain of cloud.

At the kitchen windowsill, Cous-Cous, our semi-Persian resident entertainer, is a black silhouette against the white beyond, her tail giving an occasional twitch, her topaz eyes fastened on the view of birdfeeders and the bright flash of blue jay wings. That tail and those wings are all that move in this whited-out world.

Seed catalogues began flooding in directly after Christmas, and I expose myself to their annual seductions. It has been long enough to catch my breath since the last days of harvest, and I genuinely look forward to another season of growing. There were years in which I lived where I could not garden, and in one sense I think of them as lost years. And there was one place where I tried to garden and did not do well.

We were fortunate, living in the city for the time we were working at the United Nations, to have a house that went with the job, in that section of Manhattan named for the turtles that once throve in the bay of the nearby East River. We not only had a house but also our own strip of garden, and the privilege of looking at all the other gardens which made up a metropolitan Eden in the space of a city block. Two rows of brownstone houses presented noncommital facades on parallel streets, but their back doors and windows faced on this square of greenery, each one with a diminutive private garden and all sharing in a central area graced by a fountain and a tired grande dame of a willow tree celebrated in the writings of E.B. White, who once lived here.

The distinguished ladies and gentlemen who inhabited these houses passionately loved their gardens. They would put on immaculate canvas gloves and well-cut striped aprons and stand about supervising the placement of thousands of bulbs or chrysanthemums or whatever they had ordered for the season, put in with rich dressings of peat moss and bone meal by minions of the haughty city nurseries. These householders held solemn meetings in which plans were made for maintenance and improvement of the common garden, and on summer evenings when the city was like the weight of an unwelcome lover, those residents who were for the moment not in East Hampton or Europe could be seen with their garden hoses sprinkling wilted blossoms far into the night.

There was considerable competition amongst these gardeners for the most brilliant mass of tulips in April, the glossiest vines, the most récherché bit of statuary brought home from Katmandu or Kyoto. The total effect was one of rare elegance and charm. When we had guests from the United Nations, they would come in off the filthy dismal streets and gasp with pleasure at discovering this oasis. O! they would exclaim, looking about at the patterned walks, the stone putti and outsized urns, the water flowing melodiously from the stone lion's mouth into the little pool, the perfectly groomed shrubbery and the array of weedless flowerbeds, O, it is just like a bit of London! Or Paris. Or Prague. Or Copenhagen, or wherever — but never Manhattan.

Our own private strip never came up to the standards of the others. I could see the ardent landscapers longing to get their hands on it, spend lots of money on it, give it some class. But the truth was, I did not love our garden patch. It was in a cold east corner where the soil remained clammy despite my attentions, preferring to clothe itself in green mold. Roses planted there went into decline. Tulips were so etiolated in their efforts to reach sunlight that they inevitably toppled over in woebegone rows. The only thing that flourished was the common sort of ivy, rampant along brick walls and walks.

It was always a city climate there — moist and malicious in spring, oppressively humid in summer, in the fall the still, poisoned air suffused with a sinister chrome light, in winter nastily windy and cold, or, if snow fell, the benediction of cleanliness given for only a matter of moments before the pervasive soot took over. I felt guilty, looking at the trumpet of a daffodil I'd coaxed into bloom all dingied over by the city's effluent. My heart was not in the business of making a pretend countryside in the midst of that giant forest of concrete and metal.

I only wanted to be away, far away, where the sky was wide and unsoiled and trees grew for miles without any attention from anybody at all, and gardens were open and informal and running over with vegetables as well as flowers, and hayfields rippled in the wind, and swallows dipped and glided over a pond nestled amongst hills, and the biggest building in sight was a swaybacked barn.

I have come away.

Please God I never have to leave.

During the night, snowfall, an inch or so of new blanketing. In the morning, at five below zero, sunlight so brilliant that trillions of minute prisms flashed iridescent colors wherever it reached, and shadows were cobalt. The sky an intense blue like the heart of a flame, but cold, cold. Icicles — the "fingers of January" — held their shape and even on the south side in full sun no snow slid off the roof.

After a morning at the desk, a glance at the thermometer revealed that at two o'clock it was as warm as it was going to be — three degrees above zero. So it was into parka and boots over layers of woolens and out into the dazzling air. White everywhere, undisturbed. Except for blue jays and chickadees, no life signs, no tracks. That pure expanse of undulating white — there is no way we humans can escape comparing it with marshmallow sauce and whipped cream.

By the pond, clumps of bulrushes stand half buried in snow, their blowsy heads a far cry from the sleek brown helmets of summer. Below the pond I do find life and movement — the little stream is flowing clear, making its way through the snow, a small musical note, a small indomitable movement, a small message of life in all the frozen silence.

I visit the elm, the harp of the meadow. Is it still living? Will it leaf out once more in the green of April? I press my ear to the rough trunk. There is no sound, no answer. We can do no more than wait out the allotted reign of winter.

The little panes of glass flanking the front door are almost opaque, thickly etched with frost ferns and starbursts. Breathing upon them will open a coin-sized space to serve as keyhole through which to survey the outside world.

Joseph Wood Krutch wrote that frost flowers have been around for billions of years, growing just as perfectly as they do today. As long as there is moisture anywhere and cold to chill it, frost flowers will certainly grow, cannot become extinct and cannot change.

Seated behind the wheel of the station wagon, I try to steer it behind the Bronco William is wrestling between the drifts. The two machines are connected by a heavy steel chain. William had driven the station wagon on a six-hour journey that day, to find on arrival home that our lane was impassable. He left it at the turnoff and came to the house long enough to change into work pants and duffle coat, then was out again to bring the caterpillar tractor with its massive plow sputtering to life, and to begin the heroic task of cutting through the drifts that had been piling up all day.

I had been out twice that day, morning and afternoon, to feed the horses. The journey through the snow to the barn had been an ordeal. The wind from Canada iced the air to temperatures far lower than the thermometer's minus ten degrees. Snow had drifted through the cracks into the stalls where the horses snorted and stamped with frost plumes belling from their nostrils. The pump had frozen. The only warm things in the barn were the fresh horse droppings, and the familiar fragrance of molasses mixed with oats was frozen before it could rise with the lifting of the lid from the barrel. The wind had created mountains of snow between house and barn. There were stretches where I sank to the waist, forging ahead in air so icy that to breathe was to experience a knifing in the lungs. Cheeks and nose turned to marble, and the cold penetrated instantly through all the layers of clothing with what seemed a vindictive and entirely personal attack. When I made it safely back to the house and took off gloves and boots, my fingers were white at the tips, my toes without feeling.

Now I am back out in this inhuman weather, the shrieking wind blasting cyclones of snow in the inky night. Our headlights illuminate myriads of flakes rushing past in a kind of insane whirl. The Bronco groans and sways, the chain tightens, and we move forward in lurching tandem. I am concentrating on guiding the station wagon in its narrow channel when, quite unbidden, a brilliantly lit scene flashes across my mind: A palm tree arches over a crescent of white beach, a sparkling Caribbean sea laps the sand, a burning sun blazes down from a cloudless sky. The vision is gone as quickly as it came, and I am left blinking in the reality of sub-Arctica.

But how banal — a postcard scene, reducing a whole climatic zone and culture to such stereotyped elements. And how disloyal even to think of it! I have never wanted tropical ease. I passionately prefer the challenge of sharply defined seasons and life in the rural northland. There is the keenest sort of pleasure to be earned in overcoming natural difficulties, in living intimately with austerities which call upon extreme resources of body and mind.

In today's world, it is possible, as it was not for most of our forebears, to choose to some degree the locus of our lives. We do not need to do battle with blizzards; if we wish, we can pick up and go find a job in a state where air conditioning is more important than furnaces. But what do you lose in such a trade? Perhaps a foolish pride in being able to endure the worst with which nature can test us, for one thing. A joy in the supreme beauty which is vouchsafed us in these hills, nearly every day of the year. A kind of mystery which lies behind this beauty, something I can only call an innate godliness, a presence invested with dignity which asks a like dignity from those who dwell with it, though they may not always find the strength to respond.

Once under this spell, one resists the seduction of the south, finding it too easy, too endlessly rich in warmth and fruits, too facilely claimed and exploited. It is the difference between Puritans and conquistidores. One may not really be better than the other, but the true northman will know himself alien in that softer world, and will not stay long where the living is easy.

Daybreak, even on the coldest morning, can bring the most tender baby colors of pink and shell, moving warmly across glacial expanses of white, bringing a blush to icy mountain faces to the west, imparting a roseate mantle to the entire scene, disarming those who do not look at the thermometer before venturing out into that delusively rose-hued world.

The lowest temperatures we have known here — 33 below zero on our hill, minus 35 in the village. Not a day for gadding, but we do. Two hours of patient coaxing start the automobile. On the heights traversed by the Interstate highway the mountain panoramas are crystallized beneath an utterly bare and scintillating sky. We proceed through a congealed landscape until, without warning, the heater fails and gusts of polar air fan our legs. Simultaneously, the temperature gauge on the dashboard registers an alarming rise. Clearly the engine is rebelling against performing in such weather.

The heirloom laprobes which had once graced Uncle Charlie's Pierce-Arrow are draped about the hood, Christopher and William shivering as they work exposed to the wind. Even tied down by William's deft sailor knots, the blankets luff disquietingly when we start up, although our speed is now reduced to less than ten miles an hour. The trouble, William guesses, is an insufficiency of antifreeze, although enough had been poured in the motor to take care of temperatures to 20 below; when the car moved at relatively high speed, the wind chill factor had lowered the temperature to a point where ice had formed in the gas line.

We crawl several miles, feeling ice forming in our own life lines, and turn off at an exit where there is a service station. More antifreeze is the remedy, and we are able to continue on our way. Out there in the open, we might very well have frozen to death, but now we are moving along, warm and comfortable in our magic four-wheeled box. We make it across the river to our friends in Hanover, an hour late, and gratefully accept more than one cup of Swedish glög to thaw us out completely.

All this time I find myself reflecting on the insolence of contemporary humanity, assuming our clever inventions have overcome the age-old obstacles of distance and climate. The backward vision of small bands of hirsute cavemen, eyes burning like cave fires in dark sockets, lurching in panic before the encroaching walls of ice, flashes at intervals across the white tunnels of my mind. How can we dare to think our ingenious contraptions and devices have ensured a permanent comfort and protection? We are inherently vulnerable, inherently limited by our fragile physical forms, our bodies exactly as subject — no, more so — to freezing and starving as those of our grunting ancestors. Our confidence in machines and shelters that defy the elements is as arrogant as it is pitiable. Any and all of our securities could vanish in an instant of global catastrophe, or be lost gradually as we expand our resources and increase our numbers. We have outwitted ourselves; we have forgotten our primordial bodies, and it is our bodies that will have the last word.

In January, everybody looks old, even the kids.

When the temperature goes to ten degrees below zero, we allow ourselves the luxury of a fire in the bedroom fireplace. (We would use it oftener had we a limitless woodpile and if it weren't something of a chore to bring the wood upstairs.) It is always lit with some ceremony. Seeing the flames catch and dance, feeling the warmth that radiates so benignly, we are cheered in that limbic section of the spirit that registers any momentary victory over the eternal menace of the cold. The play of light and shadows on walls and ceiling has its own fascination. We are Cro-Magnons watching spirit-forms on the roof of a cave, we are Plato's subterranean creatures trying to fathom the events of the world from a drama of shadows, we are sentimental Victorians singing a duet: *Just a song at twilight, When the lights are low, And the flick'ring shadows, Softly come and go-o-o-o.*

With two miniature glasses of Drambuie, we are further fortified against the cold that crackles at the windows and makes the old beams and rafters groan. Once under the blankets and quilts, with the firelight contesting ruddily against the ice light of the moon, we give thanks for warmth in a season when so many are cold, and for our great fortune in having each other in a world where so many are alone.

The room is ample, though its low ceiling slopes north and south in accordance with the steep roof lines. Under the eaves run two long closets which can be entered upright only by children or gnomes, but which contain lifetimes of treasures: books, luggage, old pictures, my grandmother's wedding dress, William's grandfather's top hat, a heterogenous collection of letters, a Seth Thomas clock being held for the far-away daughter whose wedding gift it was from her grandparents, children's drawings too precious to discard, paintings, and early literary works. It is ideal mouse country, but as it is regularly patrolled by the cats, mice are never long in residence.

There is another closet, of reasonable height, where our clothing is jointly lodged and a jumble of boots and shoes vie for floorspace. A dormer window looks out into the branches of the maples and beyond to the pond and the southern rim of hills. A larger window to the west gives a view of Brandon Gap and its guardian mountains.

On the floor lies the Tunisian rug brought home from North Africa. The tones are soft, mostly what is called Sidi Bou Said blue after the holy color with which the doors, grills, and windows are painted in that white-domed village overlooking the blue Bay of Tunis toward the blue mountain, Bou Kornine. There are bits of rose madder and white in the motifs of the rug, diamonds and tiny squares in one of the traditional patterns by a weaver in Islam's second holiest city, Kairouin of the 500 mosques. There is also a hooked rug of my own making, done while I was pregnant with my third child, depicting a gnarled Vermont apple tree hung with fruit as round as I felt at the time.

There are chests of drawers, one butternut, one mahogany, one bird's-eye maple with marble top, all of which have seen long service in the family, and a low cane-seated chair sits at the right angle to the fireplace for toe warming.

On the walls are family photographs, twenty or so in a random variety of sizes and frames, depicting six generations from William's great-grandfather Elisha Huntington, seven times mayor of Lowell, Massachusetts, to the youngest grandchild. Over a corner bookcase hangs a large print of Edward Hicks's Peaceable Kingdom, in another corner is a tiny painting of a Connemara cottage brought from Ireland, and, over the fireplace, a large ceramic plate made by Picasso in his old age, moulded as a slyly crazy clock face with the numerals all mixed and backwards, a rogue's curve of a mouth smiling, laughing, at the idea of time.

The heart of the room is the bed, a nonesuch of a bed. Its base is a large wooden platform with storage drawers. It is framed by four pine posts, fitted between the wide pine floor boards and the ceiling beams. These posts are sections of a hollow mast found by William after long search in a Connecticut shipyard. The mast, discarded in favor of an aluminum replacement, once carried sail for a sloop named White Waters, making its resting place here in the hills above the White River agreeably appropriate. Through the hollow sections run metal rods connecting the beams of the living room ceiling below with the ingenious truss arrangement in the attic above. Thus the bed literally holds the house together.

In the north country, the right sort of bed for the long winter nights is not an indulgence but an indispensable stronghold against forces stronger than our own, a requisite and comfort for body and soul.

Why are we always driven to comparisons? Snow glittering like diamonds; ice delicate as lace; gnarled stumps like goblins; clouds like sails. If we truly look at anything, it is not like something else, it is itself. Many before and many after John Donne have declared that comparisons are odious. Mostly they are not odious so much as lazy products of lazy minds. We simply don't take the time to view anything in depth — studyng, absorbing, learning about its distinctive individuality, whether it be chrysanthemum, fish, or dragonfly. It's much easier to make a glib comparison, to feel rather clever at discovering a similarity, rather than getting at the essence of the thing itself. I do it all the time. A metaphor, intuitive or informed, can illuminate, but all too often it is an excuse for not taking a closer look.

City children grow up nowadays without any contact with large animals. Cats, dogs, perhaps, for the fortunate. What is missing from the urban scene is what gave it for centuries a direct connection with the animal world, and a link with the rural — the presence of large numbers of horses. No city child was without the experience of seeing horses at work, drawing carts and carriages, ridden by travelers and errand boys, pulling up before taverns and inns with stagecoaches and passengers. Throughout the city there were stables where horses could be seen feeding on hay and oats, being curried and harnessed. At blacksmith shops the horses stood, their slender legs crooked in the arms of the farrier fitting them with new iron shoes. The sound of horses was everywhere, their feet ringing on cobblestones in rapid trotting or clopping in heavy pace. In hospital streets or before a house where someone lay desperately ill, hay was strewn to muffle the noise of horses' hooves. And their droppings were everywhere, tons of them swept up by street brooms but leaving dust and odors that proclaimed the nature of these indispensable beasts. A child might never get to the country, but that child would have a very good idea of a horse, and of its relationship to humanity. And it is only since World War I that these familiar sights have vanished.

All gone now. If a city child spots an occasional mounted policeman, that will be the extent of acquaintance with horses. There will be no conception of the wondrous structure of a horse, its spirit and its bodily strengths and needs. There will be no standing at a respectful distance, studying the rolling eye, the arching neck, the switching tail, and no reaching out to caress the velvet nose. There will be no impulse to run alongside a horse at an imitative gallop, neighing with joy, as any child might have done in the days before the combustion engine made Dobbin obsolete.

It is a loss indeed. What a pity to think that so many now come to the end of a narrow childhood having never known any creature larger or nobler than a cockroach.

Just perceptibly, the days are longer, and the sun, when it chooses to appear, stronger. Cous-Cous, who has a flair for finding resting spots where she will not only be comfortable but also look strikingly handsome, now reclines on the dining room table in the full morning sunlight, demonstrating the utilization of cost-free solar heat.

We wake to the unseasonal sound of rain cascading on the roof. From the window, snowscapes look sickly through a screen of water. The obliterating drifts slowly begin to disintegrate and subside, while the temperature mounts to a preposterous fifty degrees. A flock of grosbeaks congregates beneath a dripping apple tree, intent on shreds of bark and wizened fruit stored in the rotting snow.

The rain falls continuously for two days. The stained and granular layers of snow remain heavy with moisture. Ice cracks and jackknifes in the streams; dark and angry waters rise and batter the banks. At the bend where the road starts its climb out the valley, Brandon Brook has rechanneled itself, roaring through the meticulously restored old house that has stood there for years, smashing its windows, wrecking furnishings and interiors. To the north, a bridge is washed out, floodwaters flow deep across the road. It is a January thaw with a vengeance.

On the third night, winter reasserts its supremacy. Dense fog in the morning, ice coating every twig and branch, treacherous footing everywhere. Then snowfalls, two in succession, the second a precipitation of extraordinary beauty, each crystal lying separate and perfect amongst its companions, glistening, radiant. Once more we are locked in snow, and William is back to plowing again, morning and night, raising white bulwarks all along the lane.

John Greenleaf Whittier, that prolific celebrator of nineteenth century New England life, wrote in "Letter to Lucy Larcom,"

But I'm snowbound, and cold on cold, like layers of an onion,
Have piled my back and weighed me down as with the pack of
  Bunyan.
The northeast wind is damper and the northwest wind is colder,
Or else the matter simply is that I am growing older.

Candlemas Day! Candlemas Day! Half our fire and half our hay! chanted the country people of old England as February arrived. We have still half our hay, but the firewood has dwindled below the middle mark.

We were glad for two days when the cold relented. We saw once more the top courses of the stone wall beyond the kitchen window, and the brave skeletons of lilac, sarvis tree, and quince. The interval of relative warmth and calm was more than pleasant for the little creatures who have been hungering in tree hollow, underground, and in deep woods. They came forth in company, deer to orchard, birds to feeders. The rock maple became in the sunlight a tree of life, animated by blue jays, chickadees, nuthatches, woodpeckers, and the acrobatic squirrels, all flitting, darting, pecking, spiraling through the bare branches, ravenously attacking seeds, crumbs, suet.

But it was not to last. The elephant clouds massed in the west and moved in ponderously. Snow, snow, and again snow. The barometer fell beyond the bottom line. A wind rose out of the northwest with giant breath, increasing in force and ferocity to near-gale intensity. White pellets were driven across the snowfields so thick they blotted out what wan light there was.

The noise has been thunderous for a day and a night. The house quivers, cries out under the assault. Nerves twang, eardrums reverberate under the incessant roar of the wind. The house, its windows once more opaque with frost, becomes a cold, echoing chamber, a shell savaged by the storm.

Out in the fields and woods, have the birds and beasts found the shelters they left so joyfully yesterday? Are they huddled wakeful in this tempest of sound?

It is a cruel Candlemas.

At a meeting of the Historical Society, people spoke of the past of this community, revealing that although local history can boast no epics, there was plenty of endurance and good humour. Clara Woods' memory went farther back than most, and she told us of her grandmother's log cabin, and of the lively little settlement back in the hills where now only her family's house still stands in a constellation of cellar holes.

"What caused the abandonment of these homes?" I asked.

"The automobile," Clara replied promptly. "The automobile. They just drove away and never came back."

In a ten-hour storm, a million billion snowflakes may fall on one acre of land.

William Bentley of Jericho, Vermont, who devoted his life to capturing snowflakes on film, called snowflakes in a February storm "a birthday gift from kind winter" (his birthday being the ninth of February).

How long the carcass had been there, I could not tell. It could have been weeks, with the long spell of below-freezing weather. It had been well picked over, the spine and ribs exposed, the haunches gone, no eyes in the brown mask of the head twisted on the bones of the curving throat. The snow surround had been roughened and disturbed by a host of diners at this midwinter feast; prints of claws converging here left proof of visitation, and nearby fanmarks had been feathered upon the snow by wing of hawk and crow.

I had come upon this ravaged corpse unexpectedly, crossing from the woods into a sun-bright clearing. How had the end come for this doe? Had she been pursued by hurtling, baying dogs, chased through the protecting trees out into this open space, to be brought down and savaged? Or had she ventured out on trembling legs in the last search for forage, only to sink down in the final weakness of starvation upon the snow whose indifferent depths buried the grass and moss remembered from green summer? However this death came about, others were nourished by it in the impartial recycling of nature.

On this same day, standing at the sink, looking out on the bird feeder, I saw a plump little chickadee hopping from higher to lower forsythia branch, keeping an eye on the squirrels feeding on the scatterings at the foot of the maple.

With lightning speed a sparrow hawk winged in, scooped up the chickadee and without pause shot off. It was an act so swift and incisive that I could hardly believe it had occured a few inches away before my eyes. But the chickadee was gone, the forsythia sheltered no bird, and off on a mid-branch of the bare-limbed maple the sparrow hawk perched and dined, an elegant shape against the innocent blue of the sky.

I read, in a news story geared to Lincoln's birthday, that the Lincoln Memorial is succumbing to the onslaughts of pollution from the thousands of vehicles which circle it daily, as well as from the jet exhausts of the airliners which pass directly over it every two minutes on the approach path to the National Airport. The monument, I was surprised to learn, is a mere sixty years old, yet its handsome Doric columns are pockmarked and flaking. One expert describes the effect as "a very serious cosmetic problem."

Fortunately, so far, erosion has spared the statue of Lincoln, designed by Daniel Chester French to show "the gentleness, the power, and the intelligence of the man." Honest Abe was not one to worry about cosmetic problems. In an early campaign speech he referred wryly to his own "poor, lean, lank face," which he was aware did not appear sufficiently Presidential to many voters. But he well knew the character which can be discerned in human features. Once a certain candidate for an important appointive post was recommended to Lincoln, but was turned down "because I don't like his face." Reproached for what seemed an unjustified refusal, Lincoln declared that while a man can't much help the way he looks before the age of forty, after forty "he is responsible for his own face."

It is as difficult to imagine Abe in the hands of television makeup men as it is to think of his allowing a tarradiddle of speech writers to compose his public addresss. On that score, he said, "In times like the present, men should utter nothing for which they would not willingly be responsible through time and eternity."

Some of our leaders today are irresponsibly making utterances which could very well insure that there will be nobody at all around on this globe through time and eternity.

Down in the hollow the great horned owl calls in the frosty night, imperious quintuple notes repeated over and over. Is a mate listening, huddled and blinking in the dark shelter of a spruce?

If she hears, she does not answer. But the Valentine message has been delivered.

In the prolonged winters of the past, country dwellers had to live with silence. Except for domestic bustle, and the subdued noises of animals pent in barn and sheepfold, the white world surrounded them with a silence at once healing and forbidding, spacious and confining. That it did at times become unbearable we know not only from writings that have come down to us from the past but also from the words of those still living who recall a time before radio, phonograph and television. Never mind that silence, however lengthy, is preferrable to the trivia that these technological marvels can bring into the remotest farmhouse today; they can also bring music of superlative quality, a miracle for which we cannot be sufficiently grateful.

In the busy outdoor seasons, this is something we seldom have time for, but in the interior days of winter, music becomes a major part of our lives. Most particularly, Mozart becomes part of our life, for we listen to him above all others for exaltation. Mozart, whose own life was so crossed with disappointment and tragedy, kept the beasts at bay with the magic flute of his genius, saluting the joy of the world. There is nothing, for me, to equal the clarity, purity and charity of his music. Emotion quickens his work, and passion, but not despair, and what is not heard is the note of complaint.

Is it a kind of whistling in the dark? Yes, but a most glorious whistling, true in its tone, imaginative in its complexities, defying the dark with wit, gallantry, and perfection of techique. The Irish flautist James Galway, who says that as a child he used to think Mozart was speaking through him, is atune with Mozart when he speaks of his own belief that "it is every man's duty to put as cheerful a face as possible on himself. We are not here to make others feel miserable."

Mozart puts a cheerful face on the bitterest reality. His is the divine capacity to pierce the deathly silence of the soul's midwinter with a celebration of the life lying within each ice-imprisoned bud and in every root of grass now frozen beneath the immense wasteland of snow.

A roving reporter, interviewing the residents of Sutton, Vermont, on how they were getting through the winter, evoked the following responses:

"Time doesn't seem to drag in the winter, there's always plenty to do. I've never felt trapped."

"I'm having a marvelous time on my hillside. I wouldn't go south if they paid me."

"I love to snuggle up at my wood stove and read, or bake cookies and bread."

"We play a lot of games, like backgammon and Aggravation, cribbage and cards."

"It keeps our legislature honest — too cold for corruption."

"What's the point of complaining? It wouldn't make any difference."

"You know, if you brought all the leaders of the world together, and made them survive one winter in Sutton, 75 percent of the wars would never have happened. I believe they would come to the understanding, 'I'm not alone.'"

An unseasonal rain fell purposefully for several hours, long enough to reduce some of the snow sufficiently to reveal burlap patches in the fields. Then with a precipitous drop in temperature everything moist turned to ice. The pond is now a silvery-blue mirror, cracks radiating widely and now frozen over, the surface perfect for skating. I have not skated since a fall on the ice fractured my sacroiliac joint, immobilizing me for weeks. But William was eager, so down we clambered to the pond, Mr. MacGregor weaving in and out of snow pockets and frozen tussocks.

On the ice, his pom-pom cap at a jaunty angle, William swooped and circled, warbling Strauss melodies. The sun slid in and out of clouds, and a pale half-moon peered down from the blue eastern hemisphere. Mr. MacGregor stood anxiously at the edge of the pond, barking his concern just as he does when we go swimming — he clearly senses danger in our playing about in water and on ice.

I circled the pond, finding a little grotto on the bank where icicles formed a backdrop and water trickled slowly underneath with a quiet musical note. William skated over to where I paused in a thicket of reeds, and declared he was going to pull them out, for they were growing too rank and might one day take over the pond as had happened with our neighbors the Deweys. But our pond is much deeper and in little danger from a bulrush takeover. Besides, when we yanked, they proved firmly anchored in ice above and mud below. But we stripped off some of the dried muffs at their tips, the color of Mr. MacGregor's undercoat and as soft. Loosened from their cases, they escaped into the air like thousands of gossamer moths, ascending and then floating outward over the south bank of the pond, over the brambles and hackberry and into the tangled willow branches. These seeds may find their way to damp spots below and start another colony.

I followed some of them down to where the hollow torso of a maple stands twelve feet high, and examined its crumbling surface perforated with holes small and large, reading the record of generations of woodpeckers and flickers in search of the myriad insects who made this shattered column their home. High up are crevices wide enough for all kinds of tenants — owls and squirrels — and at the rotting roots, rooms for rabbits, mice and chipmunks — a democratic condominium. But though I watched and listened for some time, there was on this winter afternoon no sign of them. How happy I would have been to hear a slight stirring, to see a furry muzzle and cautious bright eye. But if there was anyone home that day, they were careful not to let me know.

So it was back to the pond, where William tirelessly etched figure eights and lifted a leg in graceful pirouette, until at last the wind rose and the moon grew brighter and the sun slipped well behind the hills, and it was time to leave the ice for the fireside.

Beverly, visiting from Philadelphia where she works with disturbed children, asks about what is done for them here. I promise to put her in touch with someone who knows more about it than I do, and we talk about the parallels and contrasts in urban and rural social problems.

We do not have the kind of crime in the streets that pervades large cities, though people have been mugged in Burlington and Rutland. We do have, for some of the same reasons, theft, vandalism, alcoholism and drug addiction, child abuse, wife beatings, incest, rape, and murder. Drunken drivers regularly slaughter people on our roads. An argument may end in one of the antagonists being shoved into the deep waters of a quarry. Arson, especially the burning of barns, is a recognized method of revenge. There is poverty and hunger here, in some places to a shocking degree, and a rural slum can be as soul stunting as one in the city.

Vermont, whatever idealized version of it may be advertised and eagerly bought by outsiders, is not heaven. But it does have a tradition of caring for its own, via state bureaucracies, church agencies, or simple neighborliness, that makes a difference, if not totally, at least to a respectable degree. Because of its small size, its absence of large metropolitan concentrations of the deprived, and what I can only call the decent instincts of a large number of its people, it has fewer of the intractable horrors that trouble the cities. While we know our answers to these problems are incomplete and inadequate, as they are everywhere, we do try to keep our people cared for and the air clean in the face of recalcitrant human nature and all the late 20th century influences that converge upon this little mountain realm, from heroin dealers to acid rain.

During the extreme cold of the past month, there were casualties in woods and fields as the frost penetrated deeper into the earth, invading burrows and underground passages where furry creatures are domiciled. For a time, even the blue jays and chickadees seemed reluctant to make any unnecessary essays into the lethal crystal air. But a pair of wild turkeys has ventured out from wherever they have kept all this time, in search of crucial nourishment. They are ignorant, or stupid, or desperate, for they pay no heed to Mr. MacGregor's barking from a line only a few yards distant — he outraged and puzzled by these grotesques that walk the ground like animals and yet can take off on clumsy wings to perch in the branches of the apple trees.

These two are descendants of the 31 New York State turkeys released in Pawlet and Castleton in 1970 to restock Vermont woodlands. Common in the days of early settlers, wild turkeys had been hunted to the point of vanishment here. Now there are again thousands of them in our hills, but still it is a rarity to see them in the open like this.

This pair goes its separate ways, the female as far as the willow and alder hedgerow by the road, the male confining himself to three or four chosen trees in the orchard. She bobs and weaves in the tangle of roots and branches, he pecks in the snow where deer have already trampled at the base of the apple trees, prying out frozen bits of apple, perhaps a few congealed buds or insects. They move with an entirely gallinaceous gait, graceless but sure. Silhouetted against the snow, they are primitive dark shapes, their elongated necks and rugose wattles having none of the shapeliness of our usual avian visitors. We have yet to see any of the spreading of tail feathers which give the turkeys a dignity and drama otherwise quite lacking. So far, they bring to mind only feather dusters, not Indian chiefs.

In the making of bread, there is a ritual and choreography of great antiquity. The woman takes the very steps, makes the very motions, of countless mothers, daughters, sisters before her. She engages in a task and a rite, both domestic and sacred, dedicated to the carrying on of life.

First comes the measuring out of the flour; feeling it soft on her fingers she will remember the sun on the fields where the grain ripened and think of the mill that ground it to this use. Then the water, chaste in its cup, receives the pungent yeast that conceals in pale morsels a miraculous vitality. The woman spoons out the honey, sprinkles the salt. Now the mixing, the circular movements, one hand working with stout wooden spoon, the other curving round the bowl braced against belly. Mingling of elements, creation of a new entity, this solidity, this substance dense with affirmation.

Now the scattering of flour upon the board, and the turning out of dough. The slapping and rotating, the shaping of the sphere. Then the joyous long strokes of the kneading, back and forth, side to side, the dough coerced into swift upendings and reversals. Feeling the push in shoulders and breasts, the woman engages her whole body, back and hips and legs, conscious of the feet gripping the floor and sustaining balance. Flexing the fingers and pushing with palms and the hard heel of the hand. The thumbs forcing their way into the resistant mass. Then a sudden yielding, a responding of the dough. The sense of yeast coming to life, quickening the grain, and the hands bearing down, lifting up, urging on this life. A communication rises between the woman and the dough, becoming lively, playful, exuberant.

When it has reached a state of readiness, the dough is taken up and placed gently in the waiting bowl, covered with clean linen, and carried to a place of sheltered warmth. It lies there unseen, pregnant, soundlessly swelling while the woman goes about her work, aware in the kitchen of her spirit of the growing and the expectancy that is happening in the bowl, under the cloth.

When at last the rising of the dough arches the cloth like the garment of a woman great with child, it is time to take it up. It is with a pang that the woman presses down this hopeful shapeliness, hears the sigh of the escaping breath, sees the instant shriveling back. So to kneading once again, this time with greater force, almost punishing the dough with sharp and serious strokes. When it has been pummeled once more into animation, it is allowed to rest. It lies for a little time only, gathering strength. Then it must be torn apart. There in the cleft dough is revealed the texture of life within, the mysterious geometry of leavening. Each portion of the dough contains its own aggrandizement. The fragments are folded over, smoothed out. Now the shaping of the loaves, the firm sculpturing into forms that hold the answer to hunger. And now the placing into strong iron pans black with a thousand bakings, and a final benedictory touch as the dough is swathed once more and left to its second rising.

In time, belling high and impatient, the loaves are ready for the oven. Quickly they are ranged, each in its separate spacing. The heat welcomes and surrounds them. The oven door closes upon them with an eager clap. The woman, having done her part, stands an instant, willing the bread to bake to perfection in the hot and private dark.

Soon, the loaves send out a message of well-being in a fragrance that blesses the kitchen, the whole house. The woman breathes it in, smiling, and glances at the clock. Near the hour, she looks in, judging the brownness of the stiffening crusts, tapping to hear the voice of the loaf. Not quite. Closing the door, she stays near the oven, making an instinctive measurement of time. She opens the door at the instant of perfection.

The odor of the bread as she takes it from the oven is powerful and beautiful; when she taps the loaves out of their pans, the odor becomes giddying. They slide onto the racks with a satisfying thump. Now they are lined up on the table, plump, a golden umber, handsomer than jewels. The woman knows how they will taste.

Now they may come, the man, the children, the friends. She is ready, she can feed them now, with the bread of love.

To be awakened by the idiot flutter and twitter of starlings in the chimney, and to be happy to be so awakened! This is a sound we do not expect until several weeks later, when it is more officially the arrival time of these annual pilgrims. It was a bright mild day, to be sure, but the view from the chimney top would have been of endless snow fields.

During the day, this precipitate pair explored their territory, often sitting contemplatively for long periods of time on widely separated branches. They converse at intervals in their nicest fashion, an almost melodic descending call that hints of romance. They can be, as we know all too well, horribly raucous, but for the moment they sound delightful. They look very sleek; clearly they prospered during their southern sojourn, and did not find the return journey too fatiguing. They have not been seen at the bird feeder, which today has been monopolized by a bustling little downy woodpecker. They must be discovering banquets of bugs exposed by the melting snow, and, I am told, they drink the sweet maple sap after nipping off the swelling buds.

Though they are not the harbingers that would have graced a Botticelli canvas, we are pleased that these starlings have come to let us know that spring is somewhere not too far to the south, is on its way, and may even, this year, come early.

The only consolation for becoming too much older so much faster than one could have imagined is that the trees one has planted are also growing, each year adding to their stature and beauty, no longer frail saplings but taking their places with increasing nobility against the sky.

Each month has its distinctive charms, but I have come to feel a special affection for February, so often maligned. For the ancient Romans, it was a month of ritual purification, and in a sense it is that for us, for there are days of such lambent purity that the soul feels cleansed and renewed. And with its earlier dawn and later dusks, its increasingly powerful sun, February gives us our first intimations of spring.

The temperature may swing from twenty below to forty above, there may be days of blizzards, the wind may roar out of the northwest to remind us that he has not yet abdicated, ice may bejewel every twig and branch and render the roads deadly. But the cold never has quite the iron grip of January, and if there are storms there are also thaws when icicles gleam and dwindle in the sun and snow slides theatrically off the roof with a whoosh and a thud. If we are temporarily snowbound, we know it cannot be for too long, and we can use the time to plan our gardens, reflecting that it is only a matter of weeks before we will be sowing the seeds. If the day be fair and windless, we can lift our faces to the sun and feel the warmth flowing into our bones, for there is no sunlight so welcome, so voluptuous, as that of February.

This is the month for glorying in shadows-on-snow in a spectrum of blues — cobalt, violet, indigo — contrasting vibrantly with the brilliance of white. And in the heart of the snow itself hides that aquamarine color that is matched only in certain reaches of the sea. The setting sun brings the alpenglow and all the cold black-and-white hills to the east are suffused with a radiant tincture of rose and coral; for a magic interval the landscape is transformed. As the sun disappears behind the darkening hills, a golden light lingers in the west with a kind of tender clarity seen only at this time of year.

It is the best of times to take to snowshoes, those clever contraptions northlanders have been using for sixty centuries. They make their own fish-shaped patterns as they take me where I could not walk or ski. Up the hillside, across the rivulets trickling in tentative runs, through the border of spruce, I make my way to the old sheep pasture, a protected place on a south-facing hill, its wide expanse of snow glistening in the afternoon sunlight. Everywhere there are tracks, evidence of intense activity since the last snowfall. Here have been, some of them until just a moment ago, deer, rabbits, foxes, weasels, mice and shrews. Their tracks branch out in all directions, crisscrossing, spiraling, zigzagging, some made in obvious haste, others vanishing mysteriously in mid-flight as if a giant had scooped the runner skyward.

In the old pastures, the skeletons of summer's weeds resist the wind. Remnants of goldenrod and Queen Anne's lace make of their death an elegant filigree with the most delicate of shadows cast across the snow. Milkweed pods are hollow shells, save for a few that still clasp whorls of silver-winged seeds yet to make their aerial journey. Crimson barberries are small exclamations of color. The elephantine rocks sun themselves, forgetting the afflictions of frost. The warmth at their feet melts the snow in a damp circle where sometimes a green blade of grass may be tricked into rising amid the dead brown spears of yesteryear.

Down by the pond, a tide of coloration is rising in the osiers that crowd its banks. At a distance, the color is delicate, but a branch closely examined is strung with oval beads of a robust iron-pink shade. As the days lengthen, their tips redden as if eager blood were being pumped to their extremeties. The swollen buds of the pussy willows burst their carapaces. And the willows along our lane by the end of the month take on an amber hue that seems to grow more brilliant by the hour. To stand beneath them, close to the boles and low-swinging branches, is to be bathed in a promise of sunshine, even on an aqueous grey day.

February has its sounds. Outside, the derisive calls of crows, the shrieks of jays, the companionable messages of chickadees, the hooting of owls, and in the orchard the snort and stamp of deer that sets Mr. MacGregor to barking. In the glens, where there are openings between snow-mounded rocks, the impatient cadences of the brook talking to itself, and in the valley the voice of the river rousing to free itself of ice. There are good February silences as well. A hushed expectancy fills the air when somber clouds press down, blotting out the hills, swelling with snow that will descend within the hour. There can be perfect quiet in the woods where snow-laden pines and spruces release their burdens and a brilliant miniature snowfall drifts soundlessly to earth in shafts of morning sunlight. At night, under a high canopy of glittering stars, the silence is unearthly.

Toward the end of the month the promise becomes ever more explicit. Frost heaves proliferate and country roads revert to primal ooze. But there is everywhere a sense of quickening, of life in myriad forms being held back and yet edging forward. The turning of the new cycle around the sun becomes more manifest each day, and we know that with all the hills and valleys beginning to be mantled in the roseate glow of awakening sugar maples, sap will be flowing by Town Meeting Day.

"...And Winter, slumbering in the open air,
Wears on his smiling face a dream of Spring."

LEE PENNOCK HUNTINGTON served with her husband on the Quaker relief team in North Africa and as a member of the Friends' delegation to the United Nations. She is the author of several books for children and young people, including *The Arctic and the Antarctic* and *Simple Shelters,* both of which were cited as "Outstanding" or "Notable" by the National Science Teachers of America. Mrs. Huntington also wrote *Americans at Home, Brothers in Arms,* and *Maybe a Miracle.* She is a book reviewer for the *Rutland Herald* and other newspapers and magazines. The 1985 hardcover edition of *Hill Song* was a Book-of-the-Month Club selection.